Mark Whitehead

The Pocket Essential

SLASHER MOVIES

PN
1995.9
.H6
W45
2000

www.pocketessentials.com

First published in Great Britain 2000 by Pocket Essentials, 18 Coleswood Road, Harpenden, Herts, AL5 1EQ

Distributed in the USA by Trafalgar Square Publishing, P.O. Box 257, Howe Hill Road, North Pomfret, Vermont 05053

A CIP catalogue record for this book is available from the British Library.

ISBN 1-903047-27-7

9 8 7 6 5 4 3 2 1

Book typeset by Pdunk
Printed and bound by Cox & Wyman

for Miriam, my kind of final girl.

Acknowledgements:

My thanks to Paul Duncan and Ion Mills for nudging this book along, to the helpful staff of both B & C Video in Reading and 20th Century Entertainment in Islington for providing the necessary carnage, to Ian Brown who experienced the 80s boom with me (and knew it was Farley Granger), to my mum and dad who didn't, and most of all, thanks to Miriam, without whose help and encouragement this book would never have made it to the end.

Contents

Contents

1. Slasher Movies: An Introduction

Randy: "There are certain rules that one must abide by in order to successfully survive a horror movie. For instance, number one: You can never have sex... Big no-no! Sex equals death, okay? Number two: You can never drink or do drugs. It's a sin! It's an extension of number one. And number three: Never, ever, ever, under any circumstances say: 'I'll be right back' because you won't be back."

Stew: "I'm gonna get another beer, you want one?"

Randy: "Yeah, sure."

Stew: "I'll be right back."

from *Scream* (1997)

They never learn. Despite countless catalogues of evidence to the contrary, teenagers in horror movies will insist on screwing around, smoking pot and going out to investigate strange woodland noises, usually while dressed in their underwear.

Whether you know them as stalk-and-slash, knife-kill, slice 'n' dice, murder movies or whether you never knew there was a term for them, the casts of slasher movies have been ignoring the same rules for more than 25 years. Victims of the conventions of one of the most reviled sub-genres of horror movies can't be expected to know any better because, to put it bluntly, as characters in slasher movies, they are there for one reason only - to be brutally murdered for the audience's entertainment.

If this sounds close to an even more controversial branch of the movie industry, that of the 'snuff' movie, it is a distinction that was not properly made until the early 80s. The earliest recorded use of the term 'slasher movie' was in the *Whig-Standard* (Kingston Ontario) 2 Oct 1975 when circulation of suspected snuff movies was discovered: 'New York City police detective Joseph Horman said ...that the 8-millimetre, 8-reel films called 'snuff' or 'slasher' movies had been in tightly controlled distribution.'

However, although we will be delving into some pretty murky waters, it never gets quite that murky, not even when the film in question is some piece of tat like *Maniac* (1980) - and that is damned murky. For the vexing question of the existence of snuff movies themselves, the best source remains Kerekes and Slater's *Killing For Culture* (see bibliography).

The slasher movie as a genre has a purposefully rigid formula, generally telling of a group, usually consisting of teenagers, who are picked off one at a time, usually in explicitly violent fashion, by a vicious killer. The killer is punishing the group either for trespassing upon its territory or is avenging an earlier wrong perpetrated by that group or a group that they symbolically represent The killing continues until the closing scenes of the film when one character is left, most frequently a girl, who after a protracted chase and struggle with the killer, finally makes a stand and kills him/her. Variations to the plotting, and to the characters are rare. More often variations relate to the locale, the reasons for the characters being there, the manners of their deaths and the killer's reason for killing them. The slasher's blueprint was John Carpenter's *Halloween* (1978), although it was the financial success of *Friday The 13th* (1980) that opened the floodgates to countless retellings of the same tale throughout the 80s. And, while they lay no claim to being the first films to portray insane vengeance-seeking killers, both *Psycho* (1960) and *Peeping Tom* (1960) can be seen as the forerunners of the slashers because of their portrayals of psychosis within ordinary, everyday people which turns them into monstrous killers.

Slasher movies according to this definition are, with few exceptions, American-made (some other countries even adopt the same formula and affect American trappings) and they tap into a specifically American form of Gothic horror. Whereas European Gothic had emerged from and drew its inspiration from the remnants of feudal systems governed by debauched aristocrats lurking within decaying castles (for Gothic think *Dracula* or *Frankenstein*), America looked back to its pioneering and puritan past, which is linked to the sanctity of home and family and the taming of the wilderness. Thus, the punishment for transgressing socially-acceptable behaviour weighs particularly heavily on the lustful, eternally-partying teens. Teens away from the watchful eye of their elders and breaching the wilderness, usually a heavily-wooded area, are trespassing on primal, murderous forces who resent such intrusions. The heroines (and they usually are heroines), who escape the onslaught and best the monster, like their Gothic counterparts, do not emerge unscathed. Even though they may be driven mad by their experiences, they do what was right, expelling the creature whose quest for vengeance has reached beyond the boundary into killing for killing's sake.

Violence And The Slasher Movies

The only slasher films to achieve critical recognition are *The Texas Chainsaw Massacre* (1974) and, the critic's favourite, *Halloween*. Both of these deserve the acclaim they received, the former because it draws the viewer into a nightmare of such visceral impact that it is a genuine relief when it ends, the latter because of its fluid camerawork and the way the shocks are constructed. Apart from these, the slasher movie often seems the least valued of the horror genre's output which in itself doesn't have a particularly high status. But while critics may judge these films on one level, the audience see them at another. Yes, the films are repetitive, gore-soaked and populated by cardboard characters too stupid to live, but they are popular for the same reasons - the best slasher movies always know where the audience's sympathies lie. A major criticism of such films is that they force the viewer to identify with the killer through their use of subjective camerawork. For example, in the 'stalking' scenes that are prevalent in films such as *Halloween*, *Prom Night* (1980), *Friday The 13th*, etc., the audience sees through the killer's eyes as they stalk their victims. Undoubtedly problematic, this raises questions that have kept a lot of academics busy. However, if the nature and fate of the killer-characters in the films are considered then the assumption of identification seems, if not invalid, then certainly questionable.

When *Friday The 13th* hit paydirt with its creaky plot and well-oiled shocks, Hollywood saw gold in the gore and a way to appeal to teenage audiences who had rarely been embraced by major studios previously. A similar boom occurred after *Scream* (1997). In the rush to produce *Friday The 13th* clones and grab a share of the action, the fact that slasher movies in general were considered by critics to be the bottom rung of horror wasn't a consideration. Influential critic Roger Ebert had already sent a letter to Paramount executives criticising their involvement in distributing *Friday The 13th*, which gives an example of the dominant critical response to the genre. In the UK, greater problems arose with concerns about the treatment of women in slasher movies. This concern was intensified by the fact that, at the height of the slasher boom, the Yorkshire Ripper, a seemingly uncatchable serial killer who preyed predominantly on prostitutes, was still at large. *Friday The 13th* had slipped through the British Board of Film Certification (BBFC) uncut, because then-director James Ferman thought the violence was 'far-fetched.' However, public concerns over cinema violence led to demonstrations, for example the picketing of Brian DePalma's *Dressed To Kill* (1981). Such reactions had an impact on the censor's opinions and many of the slasher movies released afterwards would have acts of violence trimmed, if not removed altogether.

There remains between the audience as spectator and screen violence as spectacle an extremely complex set of relations that would take up the rest of this book to even begin exploring properly. But beneath the moral panics against screen violence (and, interestingly, most often horror movies) including the 1984 Video Recordings Bill to combat 'video nasties' in the UK and Bill Clinton's attack on Hollywood to clean its act up or face restrictive legislation after the Columbine High School killings in 1997, the one point that critics don't often take into account is the sophistication of today's cinema and television audiences. It's interesting that the same kinds of criticisms aren't levelled at films such as Peter Greenaway's *The Baby Of Mâcon* (1993), or Roman Polanski's *Macbeth* (1971), both of which are excessively violent, but set in a different period to our own and based on 'classic' tales. Yet similar criticisms have been levelled at popular computer games, such as *Quake*, where the subjective viewpoint is a common device.

The conventions of the slasher that are most often singled out for criticism are, when considered, updated versions of theatrical and literary devices that have always been with us. The killer is in effect, no more than a fairy-tale ogre fee-fi-fo-fumming his/her way through the story, picking on less-suspecting characters, the ones who don't hear the 'look out behind you!' that the subjective camerawork invites from the audience. For, if the audiences do relate to the villains, then the way the films are constructed must surely strain that relationship. Slasher movies on the whole are extremely moral. A strong morality is shown in the good versus evil set-up, the constant replaying of revenge tragedies and the fact that murder never goes unpunished. In the slasher movie, despite the cult status of Jason Voorhees or Freddy Krueger and the victims' gruesome deaths, audiences know that sooner or later one character, a character that they have been aware of from the beginning, will confront and destroy the killer. If the killer returns in a sequel, audiences also know that someone else will turn up to stop the killing. If the audience is expected to relate to the killer who is it that they are relating to? Immolated child-molesters, deranged slaughter-house workers and bulky deformed thugs in hockey masks, all of whom will be ultimately defeated. One example of concern about audience responses to the slasher is that of Canadian film critic Robin Wood. Wood, whilst praising *The Texas Chainsaw Massacre,* slated the teen audience he saw the film with because they cheered as each new victim was dispatched. He probably would have witnessed the same reaction at screenings of *Friday The 13th*, or *A Nightmare On Elm Street*. Slasher movie audiences are often young and youth, as the tabloids never tire of telling us, is associated with irresponsibility. But to assume that they automatically identify with the subject of the camera's point of view rather than recognising subjective camerawork as a device seems unnecessarily insulting.

The biggest cheers are always reserved for the side of good, when they finally defeat the monster. The forces of good are not well-trained killing machines either but ordinary kids who have kept their wits about them, realised what's going on, noticed their friends disappearing and are making a stand because there is no one there for them.

Another point worth making about reactions to the victims' deaths is that either jealousy or responsibility may play a part in why the audience cheers. Again, for all the tabloid bemoaning of the loss of innocence, many teenagers may not have had sex, got drunk or taken drugs either because they haven't had the chances offered to their on screen counterparts who often tend to party like the world's about to end, or because they know better. The kid who survives the horror usually thinks more deeply about these choices, e.g. Sidney Prescott in *Scream*. They may drink more sensibly, take only the occasional toke (as a rule, nothing stronger than dope smoking usually happens in slasher world), and do not yield to their sexual desires as easily as their counterparts. Their hearts do not rule their heads and that's how they survive. The yuppies-in-peril cycle that adapted the slasher formula makes the jealousy angle much clearer (see *The Hand that Rocks The Cradle*, *Unlawful Entry*, *Fatal Attraction* and *Pacific Heights* for example). Beautiful houses, successful people - whoo, boy, are they gonna get it. The difference between this sub-genre and the slasher was that very often those who survive do so because they *have* beautiful houses and *are* successful people - they experience traumas, lose possessions and friends to the maniac, but the maniac is most often destroyed because it is represented as being part of an underclass who dares to aspire to the lifestyles of those they attack, and it is the resources of that lifestyle that will destroy them in the end. Catch Jason or Freddy killing people just so they can move into their condo! Catch Alice, Nancy or Laurie calling their lawyer for an exclusion order!

It is also worth noting that those slashers where the slasher bests what is expected to be the final girl (*Splatter University*, *Pranks*) do not have the same attraction. The endings are downbeat and feel tawdry.

Bob, Is That You?

Nowhere, other than the subjective prowling camerawork, are the conventions of the slasher movie more obvious than in the dialogue scenes leading up to a victim's demise. As well as being easily written they also act as a form of aural shorthand. Lines such as 'Hello? Is anyone there?' '(name of boyfriend/girlfriend/ person already lying dead)...is that you?' and 'Stop screwing around' (maniacs really hate to be told to stop screwing around) immediately signal that something terrible is about to happen. Usually uttered once the character has been separated from the group and within a specific locale - a darkened room, a basement, a wooded area - they receive no response other than a pointed instrument with the maniac at the other end.

Monsters

In the main, the monsters that inhabit the landscape of the slasher movie are human, to lesser or greater extent. The debased family that is exhibited in films such as *The Hills Have Eyes*, *The Texas Chainsaw Massacre* or even *American Gothic* (1985) are shown to be, no matter how dysfunctional or monstrous, reflections of the family unit as idealised by 'society.' By rendering them as monstrous, the slasher film subverts what has been idealised. They become threatening, deadly, cannibalistic, violent forces that threaten those who wander into their territory. In these films, the side of 'good' often has to become as savage as the forces of evil in order to survive. In *The Hills Have Eyes*, the 'bad' family, the cannibalistic wilderness dwellers, have the same squabbles and disagreements as the 'good' family, and their headstrong daughter betrays them by helping out the remaining members of the 'good.' In *The Texas Chainsaw Massacre*, the family still settles around the table for dinner - Leatherface even dresses up for the occasion, putting on a jacket and tie for the benefit of their guest and their moribund grandfather. While Leatherface cooks and fusses over the family home, the Hitch-hiker, the wilful son, is out ransacking graveyards, without a thought to the chances of his discovery and subsequent exposure/shaming of the family.

Revenge, next to trespass, is the main motivating force of the slasher-movie murders. Fred Krueger takes revenge against the parents of Springwood who killed him for taking their children, Pied-Piper style. Mrs Voorhees takes revenge against the camp counsellors who are responsible for the death of her son, Jason, and Jason avenges the death of his mother. (However, nobody has ever pointed out to Jason that, since he avenged that death when he killed Alice at the beginning of *Friday The 13th Part*

2, he can call it a day now.) Most of the high school and campus-set slashers (e.g.: *Prom Night, Graduation Day, Terror Train, House On Sorority Row*, etc.) are based upon the premise of someone avenging a wrong committed on them or to a loved one by a particular group.

Shouldn't We Call The Cops?

Authority figures, such as the police, teachers and parents can rarely be trusted or relied upon in the slasher-movie. They are either absent or peripheral. In *Friday The 13th*, Steve the campsite coordinator leaves the campsite while most of the murders take place, only to be killed before he can be of any help. The same goes for Paul, the counsellor trainer in *Friday The 13th Part 2*, whose return barely benefits the heroine as he spends most of the climax unconscious. The police in films such as *Friday The 13th* and *Halloween* only serve to hassle teenagers about drug-taking and offer vague warnings about taking care. It is interesting that in both *Halloween* and *A Nightmare On Elm Street* two fathers (Annie's in *Halloween* and Nancy's in *A Nightmare On Elm Street*) are police officers (Sheriff Brackett, Lt Thompson). Both of them express doubts, if not outright denials, that the murderers (Michael Myers, Fred Krueger) pose any threat to the populace and, as a result, both of them fail their daughters. Sydney's mother in the *Scream* trilogy, it transpires, is the root of all the evil that befalls her daughter and friends. It is a tradition that continues as the slasher mutated. The law fails the victims who are then at the mercy of the monster. In the cuckoo-in-the-nest/yuppie's-in-peril cycle, they are failed by the laws that must be upheld. Monsters are freed on a technicality, or they are seen to be operating within the law due to insufficient proof otherwise (see *Fatal Attraction, Sleeping With The Enemy*, etc.). Deputy Dewey in the *Scream* trilogy is an odd case in point. Although more integral to the plots of the films on a personality level (his on/off romance with reporter Gail Weathers continues throughout the trilogy), in his role as slasher-movie policeman he is sceptical, unreliable and usually gets knocked unconscious or attacked when he is needed most.

Bad Houses

While the horrors of a slasher-movie can occur anywhere, the origin of that horror is usually in a house which also serves as the place for the heroine's climatic confrontation with the monster. In later, and lesser, slashers this may not always be the case but, as with *Psycho*'s Bates house, that glowering gothic pile with the dreadful secret in its fruit cellar, many slasher-movie houses have been a focus for the evil. A bad house, a shunned place. Such places have figured in horror literature for centuries, from the Gothic tradition of the decaying mansion to H P Lovecraft, Shirley Jackson and Stephen King. American tales of terror have had a particular disposition towards evil places and the slasher-movie is no different. Prime examples are Jason's backwoods hideout littered with corpses in *Friday The 13th Part 2*, Nancy Thompson's Elm Street detached house whose basement leads directly to Freddy Krueger's boiler room in the *A Nightmare On Elm Street* series, and the spruce clapboard Texas farmhouse that conceals chaos and carnage in *The Texas Chainsaw Massacre*. In *Halloween* the Myers' house, the site of Michael Myers' first kill and now the local spook house, echoes Poe's *The Fall Of The House Of Usher* in that it is not just the building belonging to the Myers that is a decayed seat of the fear, but the 'house' of Myers, the family line, has decayed - Michael, possessed by evil, killed his sister, the parents handed over their other daughter for adoption to hide her identity and then disappeared themselves, never to be seen or mentioned again.

In the late 80s spin-off from the slasher, the more mainstream cuckoo-in-the-nest cycle, the idea is inverted and echoes the family values that were being espoused by politicians and morally-appointed spokespeople at that time. Here, the evil comes from outside and lays siege to the family home, which represents all that is good and wholesome. From *The Stepfather* (which subverted the family value ideals) to the more reactionary *Pacific Heights* and *Unlawful Entry* - the house (and in *Pacific Heights* particularly, *property*) is something to be defended at all costs. Late 90s movies such as *Urban Legend* and slasher-movie deconstruction *The Blair Witch Project* return to the original blueprint, having at their heart a derelict house as the site of past misdeeds and present fear, buildings where bloody murder is rumoured to have taken place years before. One look at these structures immediately tells you all you need to know about their history; boarded up and shunned, no good can come from entering them.

Technology

In the slasher movie, the beleaguered characters are persistently betrayed by technology, dragging them back to basics. Survival skills are at a premium for, in any situation that necessitates escape, telephone cables will be severed, car engines will malfunction, the electricity supply will be cut off. In *Halloween 5*, Michael Myers takes out an entire power grid, plunging Haddonfield into darkness and chaos. In the *Scream* trilogy, this collapse of technology is turned into a suspicion of technology where voice-transformers disguise identities and mobile phones are frequently cloned, cloaking the killer in false identities. In *Halloween*, Lynda is strangled with a phone cord and Laurie mistakes her gasps for help as another of Annie's prank calls.

In weaponry, slasher movies also achieve a technological year zero: machetes, axes, knives, pitchforks, rope, fire, water. If guns are used they are usually in the possession of the authorities and they rarely have much effect upon the killer. Guns are also less personal because people are shot from a distance (they are, however, punchier in a witty climax - witness the endings of the *Scream* trilogy). The weaponry in slasher movies ensures that the killer and the victim must be close, resulting in primal physical contact to the death. In *Halloween 5*, Michael Myers literally hammers home the point by skewering one victim to the wall with the barrel of a rifle.

The Final Girl

Several of the films released during this time are indeed problematic in their treatment of women. Films such as *Maniac*, *Don't Go In The House*, *Don't Answer The Phone* (all 1980), *Pieces, Visiting Hours* (both 1981) and *Lady, Stay Dead* (1982) are, at the very least, questionable in their politics, often representing highly misogynistic killers. These killers, while obviously unglamorous misfits as in many of the 'classic' slashers, brutalise women in a sexually degrading fashion. However this emphasis on sexual degradation was not an overt feature of the teen slasher movie. The misogynistic killers are often blatant misreadings of Norman Bates - mainly mother-obsessed psychopaths whose murders mix sex and death to an often nauseating degree. Arguably the worst offenders are William Lustig's *Maniac* and Lucio Fulci's *Lo Squartatore di New York* (aka *The New York Ripper*). Both films operate purely as showcases for their special make-up effects technicians (Tom Savini for the former, Giannetto De Rossi for the latter), conveying disturbing and ultra-conservative messages about female sexuality. Remove the effects (as the UK video release of *Maniac* did) and you are left with grindingly poor quality movies whose only purpose is to show that sexually-liberated women are 'asking for it.'

To the casual viewer, the teen-aimed slasher movie may suggest a similar agenda, yet such films raise interesting questions about the relationship of killer and victim. Carol J Clover's groundbreaking work *Men, Women And Chainsaws* (1992) and, in particular, its first chapter 'Her Body, Himself,' is one interpretation which interrogates the subtle gender explorations that such films put forward, especially in the character of the Final Girl.

Simply put, the argument against slasher movies goes that the viewer, often stereotyped as an adolescent boy, is constantly placed in the position of the killer and that the subjective camerawork used, especially in *Halloween* and *Friday The 13th*, invites the viewer to identify with the killer. However, Clover proposes that this is only the case up to a point and that point is the Final Girl. The shift in audience sympathies is complex but whereas the previous victims are, to quote Joe Bob Briggs 'dumber than a box of rocks,' characters such as Sally Hardesty, Laurie Strode, as well as Alice and Ginny in the first two *Friday The 13th* movies are resourceful, unswayed by lustful pleasures and, rather than just heroines, (which implies damsels in distress, shrieking and waiting to be rescued by men at the last minute) are heroic in the proper sense. It is they who sense something is wrong, that their friends are vanishing. These girls confront the monster for the audience and have the courage and common sense to destroy or at least subdue it. It may be Donald Pleasence who fires the final shot, but it is Jamie Lee Curtis who struggles with, stabs and unmasks Michael Myers in the last twenty minutes of *Halloween*.

2. Ten Things To Avoid

A Paranoid Guide To Surviving A Slasher Scenario

1) Asking stupid questions. Top on any survivor's list. If you find yourself having to ask the question 'Who's there?' in a darkened environment, the chances are that you really don't want to hang around for the answer.

2) Snapping twigs. Always a bad sign. Usually a preamble to certain death.

3) Windows. Anyone near a window will end up either being dragged through it, thrown through it or have something dead thrown through it at them.

4) Cats. Always in the pay of the murderer, movie cats can lock themselves inside closets in order to leap out at you just when things are at their most tense. They can also calm the most jittery-natured character to a point where they no longer remember that they've just received a menacing phone call, been followed by strange figures, have a dark secret in their past, etc. and thus make them easy prey for the bulky figure about to launch themselves from out of the shadows.

5) Cars. Cars never work. If they are working they will break down as far away from civilisation as it is possible to be. Starting a car when being chased is pointless as the engine will consistently fail to turn over. If the car does start, check the back seat - there'll probably be a maniac in it. If not, he will be on the roof.

6) Telephones. They never work either. Or you'll be cut off mid-sentence. Or someone will strangle you with the cord.

7) Bathrooms, showers, toilets. As if you needed reminding, humans are generally at their most vulnerable when naked. Likewise, outside toilets which have thin walls, allowing pointed objects to be thrust through them. Inside toilets usually have a nasty habit of concealing severed heads. When told that *Psycho* had deterred one viewer's wife from ever taking another shower - Hitchcock suggested that he sent her to be dry-cleaned.

8) Playing practical jokes. No one ever finds them funny and they usually backfire resulting in bloody revenge four, six, ten years later.

9) Drugs, rock music and premarital sex. You knew that.

10) And finally... Always give a wide berth to any kind of anniversary or significant date on the calendar, hospitals with no patients, boiler rooms, basements and heavily wooded areas.

3. Psychos: The Beginning

'We all go a little crazy sometimes'

Norman Bates - *Psycho*

It begins, if such things can be pinpointed to one exact space in time, with a derelict farmhouse in the town of Plainfield, Wisconsin on 16 November 1957. That day, police investigating the disappearance of store-keeper Bernice Worden broke into the house of local eccentric Ed Gein to discover a scene of true horror. With the exception of his late mother's room, which had been kept in pristine condition, the rest of the house displayed carnage. They found gruesome evidence of Gein's grave-robbing trips: severed heads, women's faces peeled from the skull and nailed to the wall, a skin 'vest' with the breasts still attached. In the barn nearby, was Worden's body hung upside down from the rafters, gutted and decapitated. Never confessing to Worden's murder, Gein spent the rest of his life in a Wisconsin mental institution and died in 1982. Although America was no stranger to apparently motiveless killings (H H Holmes in 1890s Chicago for instance), Gein was different. Here was a man well known in the close-knit community who, although cranky, was liked and trusted by Plainfield inhabitants. The newspapers suppressed aspects of the case, but local gossip spread the more ghoulish details. However, it was the realisation that anyone - someone whom you asked to baby-sit your children, someone whom you had known since they were a child - could be a monster that shook people.

Horror cinema, until that point, had dealt, in the main, with the notion of the monster as a foreign element. The Universal cycle in the 30s had combined great works of European literature with elements of European folklore to create monsters (Frankenstein's monster, Dracula, the Wolf-man), and in 1957 Hammer embarked upon a bloody retelling of those legends. But the monster was no longer alien, the product of a distant and menacing culture. The monster could be your next-door neighbour.

Drawn to newspaper articles on Gein, although unaware of the full horror of his crimes, Robert Bloch, a prolific horror-story writer known for contributions to the influential *Weird Tales* and his sardonic wit, rea-lised that there was a novel here. What Bloch had not been told, he recon-structed through his own imagination, giving his monster Freudian Oedipal problems then in vogue and setting the tale in a once-successful motel. His monster was called Norman Bates, and the novel was called *Psycho*.

Psycho (1960)

Cast; Janet Leigh (Marion Crane), Anthony Perkins (Norman Bates), Vera Miles (Lila Crane), Martin Balsam (Milton Arbogast), John Gavin (Sam Loomis), John McIntyre (Sheriff Chambers), Simon Oakland (Dr Richmond), Vaughn Taylor (Mr Lowery), Frank Albertson (Cassidy), Lurene Tuttle (Mrs Chambers), Pat Hitchcock (Caroline), John Anderson ('California Charlie'), Mort Mills (Highway Patrolman), Virginia Gregg (Voice Of Mother)

Crew: Director/Producer Alfred Hitchcock, Writer Joseph Stefano, Novel Robert Bloch, Cinematography John L Russell, Music Bernard Herrmann, Editor George Tomasini, Art Direction Joseph Hurley & Robert Clatworthy, Special Effects Clar-ence Champagne, Title Design/Pictorial Consultant Saul Bass, 109 minutes

Story: Marion Crane, secretary for a real estate agent, returns to work after a lunch-time assignation in a hotel with lover, Sam Loomis. Fearful about their future (her low-paying job, Sam's debts on his hardware store), she succumbs to the opportunity to steal $40, 000 after it is left in her trust by her boss. Taking the money she drives off to join Sam but fatigue and a heavy storm force her to leave the highway and take a room at Bates Motel. There she meets Norman, the strangely withdrawn man-ager, who lives in a gothic house overlooking the motel with his invalid mother with whom Marion later hears him arguing. After chatting and eating with Norman, Marion retires to her room, her mind set on returning the money and facing the consequences of her actions the next day. She does not realise that Norman is spying on her. She takes a shower but as she does so, an unknown woman surprises her and stabs her to death. Norman discovers the body and, realising his mother has murdered Marion, disposes of her body and belongings (including, unknown to him, the money) in the swamp behind the motel.

A day or so later, Lila, Marion's sister, visits Sam, concerned about Marion's disappearance. They are joined by Milton Arbogast, a private eye hired by Marion's boss to trace her and the money. After checking most of the nearby hotels, Arbogast eventually stumbles across the Bates motel where he interrogates Norman and discovers that Marion stayed there. However, Norman refuses to let Arbogast question his mother. Informing Sam and Lila of his plan to question Mrs Bates, Arbogast returns to the house when Norman is out and is stabbed to death by an old woman. Concerned that Arbogast has departed without telling them Marion's whereabouts, Sam and Lila visit the Sheriff and are shocked to find that Norman's mother has been dead for years. Suspecting the worst, they rent a room at the Bates Motel, posing as a couple. While Sam stalls Norman, Lila investigates the house. Realising that he has been decoyed, Norman heads to the house, forcing Lila to hide in the basement where she discovers the mummified corpse of Mrs Bates. Arriving at the last minute, Sam rescues her from Norman, dressed as his mother, wielding a butcher's knife.

In a deliberately glib conclusion, a psychiatrist explains that Norman killed his mother and her lover, then assumed Mother's identity, her power over him becoming strongest when sexually aroused. In a nearby cell, Norman's personality is completely overwhelmed by Mother...

Background: Sold by Robert Bloch in a blind bid to Universal for $9,000, his novel formed the basis for the icon of the modern American horror movie. *Psycho* was Hitchcock's calculated retort to Henri-Georges Clouzot's *Les Diaboliques* (1954), a black-and-white 'vanishing corpse' thriller which had enjoyed considerable box-office success overseas and earned Clouzot the sobriquet of 'the French Hitchcock' (a title later applied to Claude Chabrol). Hitchcock, ever an earnest observer of movie trends, had noted the popularity and financial rewards reaped by low-budget horror pictures then being produced by studios such as American-International, Hammer and Allied-Artists. Where many major studio productions had died at the box office (Hitchcock's *Vertigo* (1958) included), films such as Terence Fisher's *The Curse Of Frankenstein* (1957), with a franker approach to violence and shock tactics, had proved extremely popular with audiences. Paramount executives were horrified at Hitchcock's proposal, rejecting it totally until he won them round with his offer to make the movie quickly and cheaply, using mainly the small, devoted crew that filmed his TV series *Alfred Hitchcock Presents* for Hitch's Shamley Productions. Using this as leverage, he financed *Psycho* personally, deferring his director's fee, and Paramount finally relented. Budgeted at a meagre $80,000, *Psycho* made $15 million in its first year in domestic takings alone. Hitchcock had further marketed the film by issuing cinema managers with his list of instructions for its proper exhibition. Entitled 'The Care and Handling of *Psycho*' the foremost instruction was that managers ensure no one was allowed into the film once it started. The film's posters and advertisements similarly warned patrons, and there were also strict instructions not to give away the ending. Seemingly complying, tight-lipped word of mouth ensured the film's shocks remained just that. While *Psycho* swept through box offices like wildfire, there were certainly critics and public organisations who were extremely vocal against its mix of violence, voyeurism and shocks. Critics in the UK were particularly opposed to *Psycho*, including C A Lejeune, who walked out before the climax because she was 'bored by it all.' However, such responses dissuaded few cinema-goers from attending and threatened pickets by the Legion of Decency never materialised.

In *Psycho* the authorities are, as ever, misguided - Arbogast believes Marion has vanished with the money and later that Norman has dispatched her for the $40, 000. Sheriff Chambers and his wife know only the external Norman, the face he presents to the outside world, and they react with no little surprise to his mother being spoken of as still being alive. The subjective camerawork that John Carpenter would introduce into the slasher proper with the prowling hand-held work in *Halloween*, implicating the audience in the stalking of the movie's victims, is introduced in *Psycho*. For example, Marion's final moments at the Bates Motel, as she undresses to take a shower, unaware that Norman is watching her through a hole in the wall. The audience sees Norman spying, the screen becomes the hole in the wall and we, the passive watching audience, are implicated in his crime, his intrusion and his power over her in that moment.

Psycho would eventually yield three sequels. *Psycho 2* (1983) was directed by Richard Franklin (who had previously directed the Hitchcockian *Road Games* (1981) with Stacey Keach and Jamie Lee Curtis). It is set after Norman's release, when he is coming to terms with life on the outside. Murders commence once more and are revealed to be a plan by

Lila (Vera Miles again) to have him imprisoned for good. A coda reveals that another woman was actually Norman's mother. Norman kills her and settles back to life at the motel, mother and son reunited. Interestingly, the production managed to trace every prop used for the original in order to redecorate, with the exception of the shower-head (allegedly appropriated for John Carpenter's *The Thing* (1983)). Perkins directed *Psycho 3* (1986) which tells of Norman's relationship with a suicidal ex-nun whose resemblance to Marion Crane soon drives him over the edge again. A fourth, *Psycho IV - The Beginning* (1990) was directed for TV by Mick Garris and uses Perkins in linking sequences describing Norman's childhood, using *ET*'s Henry Thomas as young Norman and Olivia Hussey as his domineering mother. With each of these films, Perkins' excellently balanced and nuanced performance keeps things on the rails even when the films degenerate into knife-killing scenes. Norman remains sympathetic despite his insanity, seeming far saner than most of those he comes into contact with. A failed TV pilot *Bates Motel* (1987) starred Bud Cort (from *Harold And Maude* (1971)) as the new owner.

Psycho remains one of the most influential masterpieces of modern horror cinema. Forming a bridge between Gothic horror (exemplified by the brooding Bates house) and the coming 'splatter movie' ushered in properly with George A Romero's *Night Of The Living Dead* (1968). All points in the slasher movie can be seen to converge at *Psycho*, as much through homage and/or thoughtless rip-offs as through the concerns that *Psycho* explored. While it remains debatable as to whether Hitchcock or Saul Bass actually directed the sequence, the shower scene is much emulated, its startling montage of shots implying rather than showing the horrific nature of Marion's death. Shower scenes, with added violence and minus montage, would become a feature of the slasher. An embryonic final girl is present in *Psycho*'s Lila. Although it is Sam who saves her, it is she who has braved the old dark house and discovered the secret of mother.

Verdict: 5/5

Sadly, while Hitchcock's film enjoyed success, another equally challenging film portraying a psychotic murderer and which exposed the audience to a provocative investigation into the notion of viewing film, was not to be given such an easy time.

Peeping Tom (1960)

Cast: Carl Boehm (Mark), Moira Shearer (Viv), Anna Massey (Helen), Maxine Audley (Helen's Mother), Brenda Bruce (Prostitute), Miles Malleson (Lecherous Customer), Esmond Knight, Martin Miller, Michael Goodliffe, Jack Watson, Shirley Ann Field, Pamela Green (Millie), Nigel Davenport

Crew: Director Michael Powell, Writer Leo Marks, Cinematography Otto Heller, Music Brian Easdale, Editor Noreen Ackland, Art Director Arthur Lawson, 109 minutes

Story: Mark is a quiet young man. A glamour photographer and cameraman by day, he stalks and kills women by night. He stabs them in the neck with the extendible leg on the camera tripod which conceals a sharp spike, simultaneously filming them and their reactions. He develops and watches these films in his own darkroom. One evening he is befriended by one of the tenants in his house, Helen, whose curiosity and sympathy for him is aroused when he shows her footage shot of him as a child. This includes disquieting scenes with his father as well as a more comfortable scene where his father presents him with his first movie camera. The films are part of an extensive library of footage of Mark taken by his father to explore 'fear in children and how they react to it.' As their relationship progresses, Mark tells Helen that he will not photograph her because whatever he films he loses. Meanwhile the police investigate Mark's film studios where a body has been discovered and Mark is tailed when he goes to visit Millie, one of the models who poses for glamour photographs in a makeshift studio above a newsagents. Mark films the policeman outside. Meanwhile Helen discovers and watches one of Mark's own films. Returning from the newsagents, he catches her. Telling her that she'll be safe so long as she stays in the shadows where he can't see her, he reveals the depth of his father's research (including banks of tapes from each of the rooms, all of them still wired for sound). Mark shows her how he killed the women, not only filming them die, but filming the fear in their faces as they saw their own deaths reflected in a mirror mounted on the camera. As the police close in, Mark is unable to kill Helen, and lets her go. Through continuing his work, Mark has become his hated father. Mark achieves rest, destroying his father, his work and himself by filming his own death using the spike attached to the movie camera.

Background: Powell, who had previously worked with producer Emeric Pressburger (*A Matter Of Life And Death* (1946), *The Red Shoes* (1948)), never received an easy time from British critics, because his approach to cinema was not rooted in the social-realist documentary school that had been the predominant movement in British film since its beginnings. (Such attitudes were also the main criticisms levelled at productions of both Gainsborough and Hammer studios.) Bouquets for the film include those from the Tribune: 'The only really satisfactory way to dispose of *Peeping Tom* would be to shovel it up and flush it swiftly down the nearest sewer. Even then the stench would remain.' Whereas noted film critic Dilys Powell commented: 'Perhaps one would not be so disagreeably affected by this exercise in the lower regions of the psychopathic were it handled in a more bluntly debased fashion.' As well as the chorus of moral indignation and critical opprobrium, Powell and *Peeping Tom* fell foul of political machinations. Members of the Variety Club, the British film industry's 'establishment' and a major charity-raising organisation, feared for their chances of mentions on the honours list because of the film and put pressure on Nat Cohen, head of Anglo-Amalgamated, *Peeping Tom*'s producers and UK distributors. The film was swiftly withdrawn and Powell's career was effectively destroyed - he ended his days directing for television and making much lesser films in Australia. Unsurprisingly, the film received a far better reception from French critics and interest in Powell's work, including *Peeping Tom*, would be revived in the 80s particularly due to praise from cineastes such as Martin Scorsese.

Initial responses to *Peeping Tom* may have been prompted by the way it confronts the audience's 'scopophilia' (the morbid desire to gaze) in a situation involving acts of violence. *Peeping Tom* is full of moments where we are literally 'caught looking' in a situation where we have no defence against accusations of voyeurism. Mark's comment when first showing Helen his father's experiment, "I never knew one moment of privacy" is a line that could be spoken by any character in any movie forever subject to the audience's gaze. His victims in their most emotional and private moments are equally intruded upon. They are aware of the killer and the camera watching them and finally forced to watch themselves as they die. When Mark sits watching footage he has shot of killing a prostitute, the audience becomes one with the camera and simultaneously becomes one with the victim through the mirror (on Mark's camera).

Powell further blurs the distinction between screen and reality by appearing in the film as Mark's father (his son, Columba, plays the young Mark) and with in-jokes - for example, it was supposedly said at the time that the only way to get a decent performance from actress Shirley Ann Field would be to 'dump a corpse in front of her,' which is exactly what happens in this film.

Verdict: 4/5

While *Peeping Tom* languished, *Psycho*'s worldwide success had not gone unnoticed and soon the very studios that Hitchcock had admired for their low budgets and box-office success, were seeking to replicate the success of *Psycho*. Prime competitors in this area were cinematic showman William Castle and Gothic horror revivalists Hammer Studios, although *Psycho*'s influence would soon reach much further.

William Castle, was the movie equivalent of P T Barnum - an affectionate parody of Castle can be seen in Joe Dante's *Matinée* (1992). Castle was the man who propelled inflatable skeletons along invisible wires above the heads of the audience (much to the delight of small boys with catapults) for *The House On Haunted Hill* (1959). His *Psycho* copies did not feature such hands-on devices but *Homicidal* (1961) told the tale of nice young girl Emily (Jean Arliss) whose murderous plot to claim the family inheritance by incriminating her half-sister includes the final twist revelation that she is - gasp - her own husband. Arliss looks extremely unconvincing in drag. Castle's showmanship here is reduced to a personal appearance to introduce the film (à la *Alfred Hitchcock Presents*) and a 'fright break' before the climax of the film to allow patrons to leave and claim their money back if they were too terrified to remain (or possibly too fed up with the *Psycho* similarities to hang around having already guessed the ending).

His second venture, *Strait Jacket* (1964), tapped into the popularity of Robert Aldrich's slice of ham and Gothic *Whatever Happened To Baby Jane?* (1963) which had allowed Bette Davis and Joan Crawford to revive their careers in splendidly overblown style. Castle's *Strait Jacket* utilised Crawford's new-found popularity in a plot written by Robert Bloch. It tells of Crawford's axe murderess, newly released from an asylum after serving 20 years for murdering her husband and his lover in front of their young daughter. Returning to the family home to live with her daughter (Diane Baker), the murders start up again. Needless to say, it's all a plot contrived by her daughter to get rid of her boyfriend's stern parents, knowing that mom will be blamed. Devoid of gimmicks, *Strait Jacket* includes some graphic axe scenes and a bravura performance by Crawford enhanced by the plot's use of her screen persona. Beyond that it's standard fare. *The Night Walker* (also 1964), also by Bloch, starred Barbara Stanwyck as the victim of bizarre plots by her lawyer (Robert Walker) to drive her mad and by a private eye (Lloyd Bochner) to blackmail her for the death of her husband. Stanwyck pulls out all the stops. The film does not.

Hammer's attempts to replicate the success of *Psycho* were equally transparent. All except *Nightmare*, were scripted by Jimmy Sangster, showcasing his predilection for vanishing corpses, mechanical plots with copious red herrings and twist endings that may surprise but often seem contrived in their machinations. They were entertaining but often slow and forgotten about almost as soon as they were over. Of these, *Taste Of Fear* (1960) and *Nightmare* (1963) are the most enjoyable, but Hammer's speciality remained retellings and reworkings of more old-world horror motifs. The rest of the series, *Maniac* (1962), *Paranoiac* (1962), *Fanatic* (1964, aka *Die! Die! My Darling*), *Hysteria* (1964), *The Nanny* (1965), *Crescendo* (1969) and *Fear In The Night* (1971), are various reworkings of Sangster's themes.

A name that should be mentioned is that of Herschell Gordon Lewis. Beloved of gore-film aficionados, it is arguable that he can be credited with single-handedly creating the gore-movie genre because his films brought to drive-in theatres the pleasure of torn-out tongues and lopped-off limbs as far back as *Blood Feast* (1963). Lewis is the godfather of the splatter movie. Creator of such opuses as *The Wizard Of Gore* (1968) and *The Gore-Gore Girls* (1971), Lewis started out making nudie flicks in the 60s but, influenced by Hitchcock's *Psycho* and pragmatic enough to know that, on his budgets, he could never afford high production values or name casts, Lewis set out to draw audiences by showing them something that they had never seen before. His entire oeuvre remains banned in the UK, which is a pity, because despite their excessive gore and problematic treatment of women they are, for the most part, a continuation of the grand guignol tradition, delighting in pain and extreme violence, and puritanical in their morality. They are better balanced than many mainstream Hollywood slashers such as *Fatal Attraction* or *Basic Instinct*. Despite rumours of *Blood Feast 2*, these days Lewis no longer directs but contents himself with writing self-help business books.

Giallos

Hitchcock's shadow fell most heavily across the Italian *giallo* films which came to prominence in the mid-60s. Their name comes from the pulp crime tales published predominantly in Italy in yellow jackets (in much the same way that Penguin books used to give crime novels green covers). The films invariably featured a faceless killer whose gruesome (and often sexually-motivated) crimes will, despite the tribulations of the hero/heroine, lead to the villain's unmasking and often suitably fitting execution. To cover the *giallo* satisfactorily would take the rest of this book but the two directors who brought the genre to greater attention, as well as having a major influence on the slasher movie, were Mario Bava and Dario Argento.

Bava, a former cameraman, brought an intense visual style to his films which became increasingly plotless and scriptless as his career as a director progressed. For his films this was rarely a handicap as the audience was not expected to relate or even understand the characters that they saw in his films but be caught up in the sheer delirium that was attendant in the visuals alone, rendering them a pure cinematic spectacle. His fantasy films include his debut, *La Maschera Del Demonio* (1960, aka *Black Sunday*) and the astounding *Lisa E Il Diavolo* (1972, aka *Lisa And The Devil*) which was butchered by the producer. Cashing in on the international success of *The Exorcist*, the producer intercut ludicrous possession sequences and re-released it as *House Of Exorcism* in 1974. Bava's *giallo* works include *Sei Donne Per L'Assassino* (1967, aka *Six Women For The Murderer, Blood And Black Lace*) and *Ecologia Del Delitto* (1971, aka *Antefatto, Blood Bath, Bay Of Blood,* etc.). In these the characters are, much like the slashers, there to be killed. Bava choreographs the deaths as if the films were symphonies.

In *Sei Donne Per L'Assassino*, Eva Bartok runs a fashion house which also fronts a drug ring. Cameron Mitchell is the handyman, who stalks and sadistically murders the models. Unlike *Psycho*, Mitchell has no mother to take the blame for his crimes. Instead Bava forces the audience to confront male sexual desires at their most destructive. Unlike *The Texas Chainsaw Massacre* or *Friday The 13th Part 2* onwards, he does not provide the male audience with the get-out clause of the killer being somehow sub-human. Masked during his killings, our viewpoint is the subjective stalking of the models - Mitchell represents pure misogyny. The women are embodiments of male desire and their deaths are Mitchell's panicked attempts to exorcise that desire by destroying successive desirable women (an impossible, endless task) which results in his own destruction.

Ecologia Del Delitto, a profound influence on *Friday The 13th Part 2* in particular, does not offer any psychological explanation for the thirteen murders that occur, nor does it offer one psychopath to take the blame. The brutal killings all happen because of desire for the bay, an exceptional piece of real estate. With exception of the countess who owns the land (killed in the opening minutes by her husband)) and her neighbours, Paolo and Anya (who both die for witnessing other murders), everyone kills at least one other person. In the end, the two survivors are shot dead by their children, who believe a gun they've found is a toy. While the film attempts to construct a 'symphony of violence' on screen, this doesn't quite come off. However, the daisy chain of killings motivated by greed remains particularly audacious.

Former film critic and sometime screenwriter (he worked on Sergio Leone's *Once Upon A Time In The West* (1968)), Dario Argento's debut feature *L'Uccello Dalle Piume Di Cristallo* (1970) (aka *The Bird With The Crystal Plumage*, *The Gallery Murders*) employed not only Hitchcock-style shock mechanics and *Psycho*-style plotting but also the visual panache that Mario Bava had brought to horror from 1960 onwards. It is a tale of a Jack-the-Ripper-style murderer at large in 70s Rome. With the raincoated, leather-gloved killer at large, Tony Musante plays a journalist who witnesses a struggle in an art gallery between a woman (Eva Renzi) and her husband (Umberto Raho), which ends with Renzi knifed in the stomach. The husband immediately falls under the suspicion of the police, and the killings continue, including attacks on Musante and his girlfriend (Suzy Kendall). At the climax, the masculine killer is revealed to be Renzi, Musante having misseen the attack in the art gallery. It is beautifully photographed by Vittorio Storraro and has a jangling Ennio Morricone score.

L'Uccello Dalle Piume Di Cristallo's successor *Quattro Mosche Di Velluto Grigio* (1971, aka *Four Flies On Grey Velvet*), by reducing plot and shaping around a succession of artistically filmed and engineered shocks, paved the way not just for *Halloween* but many future major Hollywood horror and action films. Argento's later films, most notably *Profondo Rosso* (1975, aka *Deep Red*), *Suspiria* (1976), *Inferno* (1980) and *Tenebrae* (1982, aka *Unsane*) would continue to erode plot in favour of increasingly baroque gore set pieces to impressive effect.

American Variations

Bava's and Argento's films were admired and copied by many and, in America, a prime example is Bob Clark's *Black Christmas* (1973), a film that refuses the audience even the comfort of unveiling the killer in the closing reel and reveals its influences, particularly in the killing of Margot Kidder's Barbara with a glass unicorn. The film is set in a sorority house closing for Christmas, so initially nobody notices that girls are disappearing. *Black Christmas* can be said to form the template for the slasher movie with its well-woven tale of an unseen killer, subjective camerawork, sexuality punished, urban legend, powerless authority figures and terrified teens. A well paced slasher with a fine cast: Olivia Hussey is Jess, her abusive boyfriend Peter is played by Keir Dullea, John Saxon as the sympathetic police lieutenant, Art Hindle is Clare's bewildered boyfriend and James Redmond is her prudish but stalwart father. *Black Christmas* exploits its chilly Canadian locale and, the (then original) twist of the killer's bestial obscene phone calls coming from inside the house (a device later used in more hurried style in *When A Stranger Calls* (1979)). Leaving Jess tranquillised in the house after Peter's death, the bodies in the attic undiscovered and the authorities satisfied, the phone begins to ring once more...

Clark, who had previously directed *Dead Of Night* (1972), an oddly affecting Vietnam-vet zombie movie and *Children Shouldn't Play With Dead Things* (1973) a broad zombie black comedy, went on to direct the Jack the Ripper Masonic-conspiracy thriller *Murder By Decree* (1978) and then lost it completely with *Porky's* (1982) and *Porky's II* (1983), the tits 'n' bums equivalent of the *Friday The 13th* sequels, both huge successes at the box office.

In 1974, Clark's associate on *Dead Of Night* and *Children...*, Alan Ormsby would contribute the screenplay and co-direct (with Jeff Gillen) another defining moment - the pseudo-documentary of the life of Ed Gein. In *Deranged*, the character is called Ezra Cobb (a serene childlike performance from Roberts Blossom, who would later play the scary/sympathetic old man in *Home Alone* (1990)), but the crimes are as diluted as in *Psycho*. Grave-robbing, necrophilia and cannibalism are given full range, treated in a 'true-crime' fashion, complete with authoritative narrator Les Carlson (who was the phone engineer who realised the terrible secret in *Black Christmas* and would later play the power-hungry cable-station owner Barry Convex in David Cronenberg's *Videodrome* (1982)). However effective *Deranged* was, and its blackly comic recreation of the private world of a maniac remained unchallenged until *Henry: Portrait Of A Serial Killer* (1985), it was overshadowed that same year by the appearance of another independent movie with a title that would become a model for low-budget horror and slasher movies in general, *The Texas Chainsaw Massacre*.

4. The Return Of The Repressed

'My family's always been in meat,'
The Hitch-Hiker - *The Texas Chainsaw Massacre*

The film which you are about to see is an account of the tragedy which befell a group of five youths, in particular Sally Hardesty and her invalid brother Franklin. It is all the more tragic in that they were young. But, had they lived very, very long lives, they could not have expected nor would they have wished to see as much of the mad and the macabre as they were to see that day. For them an idyllic summer afternoon drive became a nightmare.

The events of that day were to lead to the discovery of one of the most bizarre crimes in the annals of American history...

The Texas Chainsaw Massacre (1974)

Cast: Marilyn Burns (Sally), Allen Danziger (Jerry), Paul A Partain (Franklin), William Vail (Kirk), Teri McMinn (Pam), Edwin Neal (Hitch-Hiker), Jim Siedow (Old Man), Gunnar Hansen (Leatherface), John Dugan (Grandfather)

Crew: Director/Producer Tobe Hooper, Story/Screenplay Kim Henkel & Tobe Hooper, Cinematography Daniel Pearl & Tobe Hooper, Music Tobe Hooper & Wayne Bell, Editors Sallye Richardson & Larry Carroll, Art Director Robert A Burns, Production Manager Ronald Bozman, Narration John Larroquette, Make-Up Dorothy Pearl, Grandfather's Make-Up W E Barnes, 83 minutes

Story: After checking on their grandfather's grave following reports of desecrations, Sally, Franklin and their friends Jerry, Pam and Kirk drive on to visit Sally and Franklin's grandparents' house. After picking up a hitch-hiker, who they eject from the van when he cuts Franklin, and a brief stop at a gas station where the attendant tries to dissuade them from going further, they finally reach the derelict house.

Going into a nearby house to ask for petrol, Kirk's path is suddenly blocked by a huge man wearing a face patched together from dead skin. The man clubs him with a sledgehammer and drags him away. Pam follows and falls into a room decorated/littered with bones, human and otherwise. Trying to flee, Leatherface catches her too and hangs her by her neck on a butcher's hook while he continues to cut up Kirk's body with a chainsaw. Almost night, Jerry goes looking for them and, entering the same house finds Pam inside a freezer, not yet dead. He is killed before he can help.

Unable to leave because Jerry had the car keys, Sally and Franklin go looking for the others. Leatherface kills Franklin and chases Sally through his house and to the gas station. There, the old man calms her down before beating her unconscious and taking her to the family's house. She awakes to find herself tied to an armchair (the arms are human) and a guest of the family. After being berated by the old man for torturing Sally, the hitch-hiker suggests that they should let Grandpa kill her as "he's the best." Unfortunately, grandfather is so feeble he can barely even hold the hammer and, after a couple of half-hearted blows, the now-untied Sally escapes. Chased by both brothers she reaches the main road where the hitch-hiker is flattened by a truck. Pursued by Leatherface, the driver brains him with a wrench, making him fall on his chainsaw. Sally escapes in a passing van and the film ends with the now revived Leatherface whirling his chainsaw in the empty air.

Background: As brutal as the above summary sounds, nothing can really prepare you for viewing the film for the first time. The truck running over the hitch-hiker at its climax is an apt metaphor for the viewer's emotional state after witnessing the onslaught that has taken place on screen. It's based, liked *Psycho* and *Deranged* on the crimes of Ed Gein, but this time spread through an entire family. From its opening flashlight shots of rotting limbs and the sounds of digging to its final frames of Leatherface swinging the revving chainsaw against a blood-red sunrise, *The Texas Chainsaw Massacre* remains, along with George A Romero's *Night Of The Living Dead*, one of the most revolutionary and influential films in modern horror cinema. As such, it is echoed in almost every slasher movie since. There are a few movies that have come close to its original power and all too many (*Slaughterhouse* (1988), *Lunchmeat* (1987), *Just Before Dawn* (1981), etc.) are merely pale imitations. Wes Craven's *The Hills Have Eyes* (1976) perhaps comes closest to matching the power of the original, but Craven's interests lie in a different direction from Hooper's. Both are considerations of the family as monstrous but whereas Craven's self-confessed 'white-bread' family must revert to savagery in order to survive the savagery of the degraded family of cannibals that attack them, Hooper's good family are consumed by the bad, either literally or through madness caused by the encounter. The *Chainsaw* teenagers are wholesome, upwardly-mobile, and employed. The family of cannibals are degenerate, and unemployed as a result, it is suggested, of increased mechanisation in an industry where previously they were considered professionals. In one scene, Grandpa's credentials are laid on the line by the old man: "You just hush, it won't hurt none. Grandpa's the best killer there ever was. Why, it never took more than one lick, they say. Did sixty in five minutes once." Thrown on the scrap heap by the march of capitalism, the family continue to survive by clinging to its basic tenet that you must feed off others. In their case, literally.

But if the family are portrayed as having crossed the line, their domesticity remains familiar. From the outside their house and garden look well cared for - with a patch of sunflowers near the front door and a swingchair by the porch. The interior of the house may be surreally decorated with human remains but it is with a decorator's eye: the human-arm lamp holder, the 'arm' chairs, the lampshade made from faces. The old man (who acts as the father of the group) berates the hitch-hiker for leaving his brother alone, particularly for the damage he has caused ("Look what your brother did to the door. He's got no pride in his home") and the chance that he may not have caught all of the intruders which would mean discovery. Leatherface attempts to fulfil the role of the absent mother, staying at home while the others are out providing. His frantic search for further intruders after Jerry has been discovered and the way he fiddles with the edge of his apron in one scene before being told to "Get back in the kitchen" are, while monstrous, quite affecting touches. As is evident, the humour in the film is inextricably tied to its horror but what laughter might come is not easy. The 'bad' family's arguments and loyalties are mirrored in the 'good.'

Perhaps the most surprising thing about seeing the film a second time is how little is actually shown - the acts of violence are on display but blood and effects are not. Hooper's restraint in this aspect is a lesson that few following in his footsteps took on board.

Shot on a shoestring budget over a series of weekends, the Texas heat (reaching 100 degrees much of the time) as well as the physical and psychological exertions of the film, took their toll on many of the cast. Hansen relates that the atmosphere on the set became as strained as on the screen ("Nobody much wanted to hang with me") and Neal felt that, "I was coming apart psychologically." The strains put on the cast resulted in several of them refusing to work with Hooper again.

The Texas Chainsaw Massacre premiered in the UK at the Edinburgh Festival and the following year at the London Film Festival. Despite receiving strong (albeit shaky) praise, the film was refused a certificate by the BBFC and was only shown in Britain as a result of the GLC (Greater London Council) awarding it an X certificate, for screenings within its area. Some local club cinemas also showed the film. Despite its distributors attempts to allow the censors to go through the film and delete scenes they felt unacceptable, it remained exactly as powerful as before, because its atmosphere of terror pervades the whole film. It had a brief release on video but was withdrawn when there was a blanket ban on all films containing the word 'Chainsaw' in their title. (This explains, should anyone be wondering, why Fred Olen Ray's appalling *Hollywood Chainsaw Hookers* appears on the video case with a drawing of a chainsaw rather than the actual word.) It remained banned from general release until 1999 when the new BBFC head, Andreas Whittam Smith granted it an 18 certificate with no cuts. It has since been re-released on video in the same form.

Verdict: 5/5

The Texas Chainsaw Massacre has sporadically produced sequels. Of these, the best is *Texas Chainsaw Massacre Part 2* (1986). Also directed by Tobe Hooper, it's more of a parodic remake than a follow-on. The family (now cutely named the Sawyers) has regrouped, living in a cavern under a theme park. Jim Siedow is the only returning cast member, still barbecuing but also winning state-wide chilli contests. Featuring Dennis Hopper as a Texas Ranger sworn to avenge his murdered relatives and Caroline Williams as a disc-jockey whom Leatherface takes a liking to, the whole thing ends in carnage, with Williams the only seeming survivor. The relationship between man and tool is knowingly explored when, after Leatherface has caressed the insides of Williams' thighs with his chainsaw, he is unable to start it up again. Ahh.

New Line stepped into the franchise arena with *Leatherface: Texas Chainsaw Massacre III* (1990) with Viggo Mortensen as the head of the clan and a script by David Schow. It has nothing to offer other than a scene where Leatherface is constantly buzzed 'error' by his spelling game for typing 'FOOD' beneath a picture of a boy. *The Return Of The Texas Chainsaw Massacre* (1994, aka *Texas Chainsaw Massacre - The Next Generation*) is truly abominable. Directed and written by Kim Henkel (obviously desperate), it's an attempted remake which fudges every scene it steals from the original, turns into a screaming contest between everyone on screen, and has Leatherface dressing in drag to find his feminine side. Allegedly suppressed by its then fledgling stars, Matthew McConaughey and Renée Zellweger, it surfaced on video in the UK in 2000. They didn't try hard enough.

Marilyn Burns returned in Hooper's next venture, the bigger-budgeted *Death Trap* (1976, aka *Eaten Alive*) which starred Neville Brand as an insane hotelier who kills his victims with a scythe and/or feeds them to his pet alligator (who eventually gets him, too). More overblown in its plotting and characterisation, it was filmed on a remarkable sound-stage set and despite attempts by other directors (George A Romero's *Creep-*

show (1983), Roy Ward Baker's *Tales From The Crypt* (1973) and *Vault Of Horror* (1972)), it is the closest cinema equivalent of an EC horror comic ever reached. Hooper would direct one more film of interest, *The Funhouse* (1981) before beginning a slide into oblivion. This was aided by him working with Steven Spielberg on the hybrid *Poltergeist* (1982), the most financially successful horror movie made in which no one dies.

Before the next major step towards the slasher, there were two films that aided the genre's conception. The first was *Massacre At Central High* (1976), the second Wes Craven's *The Hills Have Eyes* (also 1976). *Massacre At Central High* avoids a focus on mechanical teen-slaughter by closely observing the alliances and ostracisms that are part of high school existence. Arriving at a new school, David (Derrel Maury) finds old friend Mark (Andrew Stevens) now hangs with a group of bullies who dominate the other pupils. When David refuses to join them at his friend's request, they take their revenge by crippling him. He retaliates, causing their deaths. Life at Central High settles down until other pupils begin to seek David's assistance in taking over the run of the place. He resigns himself to further deaths and plans to blow up the school. The film's sheer nihilism and acceptance that nothing ever changes separates it from the impending deluge of teen slasher movies where deaths are the *raison d'être*. With echoes of the 50s teen rebel movies of American-International Pictures, *Massacre At Central High* occupies an area that remained virtually unexplored in high school pictures until Michael Lehmann's *Heathers* (1989), whose own nihilistic ending was blunted by studio interference.

Formerly a humanities lecturer, Wes Craven drifted into film after working on a student project - when other sources dried up, he turned to odd jobs to keep himself solvent. At 31, his future uncertain, he met up with a young producer Sean S Cunningham and together they made a cheap, pseudo-documentary porn movie, *Together* (1971). It did well enough at the box office for their financiers, Hallmark Releasing Corporation, to ask them to come up with the idea for a low-budget 'no-holds barred horror movie.' The film, originally released as *Krug And Company* in July 1972, was re-released the same year under the title *The Last House On The Left* - a title that Hallmark selected supposedly as a reference to *A Clockwork Orange* (1971). It was an immediate success in the US where critics (although by no means all) gave it a good reception. Its strong subject matter meant that it was banned outright in the UK, where it remains banned to this day. The film tells the story of two teenage girls who are abducted by four thugs, led by Krug (David Hess, who returned to the role in Ruggero Deodato's *The House On The Edge Of The Park* (1981)), who rape, torture and kill them. Later the thugs unwittingly arrive at the house of the parents of one of the girls and, when their secret is revealed, the parents exact a revenge as bloody and painful as the death suffered on the girls. Loosely based on Ingmar Bergman's *The Virgin Spring* (1960) Craven, to his credit, never allows the scenes of violence to become desensitising and never plays them for entertainment value (as in the similarly-themed *Death Wish*). During the parents' revenge scenes the disgust they feel with themselves for being brought as low as their daughter's killers is made abundantly clear. These scenes, despite the killers' unpleasantness, are as protracted to watch as the girls' deaths. That said, *Last House On The Left* remains a dispiriting and deeply discomfiting film to watch. As with *Henry: Portrait Of A Serial Killer*, the violence challenges our acceptance of its portrayal for entertainment purposes in other films and, unlike more self-important 'art' movies such as Michael Haneke's *Funny Games* (1997), hits its audience right where it hurts.

After Craven had broken with Cunningham as part of his attempt to avoid the label of 'horror movie director' he found himself on the edge of poverty once more. At the suggestion of director Peter Locke, whom Craven was editing for at that point, he took on another horror project with Locke acting as producer: *The Hills Have Eyes* (1977). An update of the Sawney Bean legend (a family of cannibals who preyed on travellers in 17th century Scotland), a 'white-bread' (Craven's term) family are on a camper holiday when they break down in the desert. They are besieged by a mutant family living in the hills, several of them are killed and their baby is abducted (for the purpose of eating). The survivors fight back with a savagery equal to their attackers'.

Undeniably powerful, *The Hills Have Eyes* almost succeeds in its mirroring of the two families: 'good' versus 'evil.' While the violence is less intense than in *Last House On The Left*, it detracts from the film's mirroring effect in that, even though the 'nice' family must resort to similar savagery, the 'evil' family are more cartoonishly nasty rather than genuinely vicious like Krug, so their deaths are not so easy to relate to. In fact there is a certain silent movie satisfaction in watching one baddy (uniquely featured Michael Berryman) being torn apart by the vengeful family dog. It was to yield one sequel, *The Hills Have Eyes Part 2* (1984) which dropped the mirrored-family idea, becoming another *Friday The 13th* clone. Also directed by Craven, he admitted with some justification: "I hadn't worked in three years - I would have directed *Godzilla Goes To Paris*."

While *Hills Have Eyes* was making a tidy profit, providing Craven with an opportunity to try less overtly violent projects, director John Carpenter was being approached about the film that was to make his name in genre movies, the slasher in particular.

Halloween (1978)

Cast: Donald Pleasence (Loomis), Jamie Lee Curtis (Laurie), Nancy Loomis (Annie), P J Soles (Lynda), Charles Cyphers (Brackett), Kyle Richards (Lindsey), Brian Andrews (Tommy), John Michael Graham (Bob), Nancy Stephens (Marion), Arthur Malet (Graveyard Keeper), Mickey Yablans (Richie), Brent Le Page (Lonnie), Adam Hollander (Keith), Robert Phalen (Dr Wynn), Tony Moran (Michael, Age 23), Will Sandin (Michael, Age 6), Sandy Johnson (Judith Myers), David Kyle (Boyfriend), Peter Griffith (Laurie's Father), Nick Castle (The Shape), Jim Windburn (Stunt)

Crew: Director/Music John Carpenter, Producer Debra Hill, Writers John Carpenter & Debra Hill, Cinematography Dean Cundey, Panaglide Ray Stella, Editors Tommy Wallace & Charles Bornstein, Production Design Tommy Wallace Make-Up Erica Ulland, 91 minutes

Story: Halloween 1963, Haddonfield, Illinois. After making love to her boyfriend, Judith Myers is stabbed to death by an unseen intruder. On leaving the house, the killer is unmasked by Judith's parents - it is her 6-year-old brother, Michael.

Fifteen years later, on Halloween Eve, Michael escapes from Smiths Grove Mental Institution steals the car of his psychiatrist, Sam Loomis and heads back to Haddonfield.

Halloween. Teenagers Laurie, Annie and Lynda prepare for their evening. Laurie thinks she is being followed, which her friends tease her about, putting it down to her not having a boyfriend. She and Annie are baby-sitting that evening, across the road from each other. Laurie with Tommy and Annie with Lyndsey. Annie's boyfriend Paul has been grounded, but Lynda and boyfriend Bob arrange to visit Annie for somewhere to make out.

Having warned Sheriff Brackett of Michael's imminent arrival, Loomis visits the local graveyard to find that Judith Myers headstone has been stolen. Finding evidence that Michael has revisited his old house, Loomis awaits his return and gets Brackett to warn his men of Michael's inhuman nature.

That night, Laurie ends up sitting for both Tommy and Lyndsey, so that Annie can pick up Paul. As Annie gets into her car, she finds Michael waiting for her. Tommy is convinced that 'the boogeyman' is at large, especially when he sees Michael carrying Annie's body back into Lyndsey's house. But Laurie sees nothing. Lynda and Bob arrive at Lyndsey's house and, finding it empty, take advantage of the situation. Bob is killed and Michael, disguised as Bob disguised as a ghost strangles Lynda as she phones Laurie. Dismissing the call as a prank and then becoming more concerned Laurie crosses to Lyndsey's house and finds Annie, Bob and Lynda all dead. Attacked by Michael, she escapes but her cries for help are ignored by the neighbours as a Halloween prank. Back at Tommy's, Tommy lets her in, but Michael is already inside. They struggle and she stabs him, only for him to revive shortly afterwards, forcing Laurie to hide in a closet which he destroys. She stabs him again and, thinking him dead, she sends the children out to get help. Michael revives once more and, as they struggle, Loomis, alerted by the children, bursts into the house and shoots Michael, throwing him through the window and down into the backyard. A distraught Laurie asks Loomis if her attacker was the boogeyman. He confirms it was, but when he looks out of the window, the body has vanished.

Background: Hired on the strength of his previous work, SF-spoof *Dark Star* (1974) and urban western *Assault On Precinct 13* (1976), by executive producer Irwin Yablans, *Halloween* was originally called *The Baby-sitter Murders*. Yablans eventually hit on the idea of setting the film at Halloween night and retitled the picture with this in mind. Carpenter and his producer/co-writer Debra Hill jumped at the project, seeing it as an opportunity to make something different. Carpenter drew from his own cinematic influences, particularly *Psycho* and Argento's *gialli*.

"You know," says Sheriff Brackett, after lunging into frame to terrify Laurie, "It is Halloween. I guess everyone's entitled to one scare." If only. *Halloween* remains the archetypal scary movie, where director John Carpenter and the audience know that surprises combined with shadows are just as important as the events themselves. Michael Myers may be a killer but, in embodying Halloween, he seems as keen to scare people as he is to murder them. *Halloween* is a beautifully visualised and cine-literate film. Carpenter constantly plays with the Panavision framing of the film - Myers himself doesn't seem to exist outside of the frame and is constantly lunging into shot to make people jump when, in reality, he would have been visible ages before. This playfulness extends to the references in the film, particularly those derived from (as opposed to derivative of) *Psycho*. Capable of giving *homage* a good name, Carpenter cast Janet Leigh's daughter, Jamie Lee Curtis as the heroine which seems only fair, seeing how shoddily Hitchcock treated her mother's character. The old

Myers' house, derelict but still the seat of evil, nurses nothing worse than a still-warm, half-eaten dog ("He got hungry") and a drainpipe that smashes through the window scaring the beejesus out of both police and psychiatrist. Pleasence's character is named after Leigh's boyfriend and like him he remains on the fringes of the action until the climax when the heroine has done everything in her power to halt the evil. All the talk of the 'boogeyman' throughout the film, whilst suggesting that Michael might have supernatural powers, misses one point: why did he wait so long? Did it take the sale of his old, dark house to finally stir him, setting him off again now that his territory was threatened? Or is it that he is indeed possessed by an unspeakable evil? It's always worth watching *Halloween* one more time to try to decide.

Unlike many others of the genre, *Halloween* remains re-watchable. Admittedly the obvious shocks dull after the first viewing or so, but the film does not, continuing to supply suspense and thrills. The performances are nicely judged, particularly Pleasence's doomsaying Loomis, who manages to stay just this side of parody with his speeches about Michael's 'evil,' and Curtis' vulnerable but strong-willed Laurie. Carpenter also, unfortunately, reintroduced audiences and film-makers to the device of seeing the victims through the killer's eyes. However, the subjective camerawork is used many times to fool the audience into thinking that something dreadful is going to happen when, more often, it doesn't. This device was to be adopted and used in almost every slasher movie that jumped on the *Halloween* bandwagon from *Friday The 13th* onwards.

Verdict: 5/5

Friday The 13th (1980)

Cast: Betsy Palmer (Mrs Voorhees), Adrienne King (Alice), Jeannine Taylor (Marcie), Robbi Morgan (Annie), Kevin Bacon (Jack), Harry Crosby (Bill), Laurie Bartram (Brenda), Mark Nelson (Ned), Peter Brouwer (Steve Christy), Rex Everhart (Truck Driver), Ronn Carroll (Sgt Tierney), Ron Millkie (Officer Dorf), Walt Gorney (Crazy Ralph) Ari Lehman (Jason)

Crew: Director/Producer Sean S Cunningham, Writer Victor Miller, Associate Producer Steve Miner, Cinematography Barry Abrams, Music Harry Manfredini, Editor Bill Freda, Art Director Virginia Field. Special Make-Up Effects Tom Savini, 95 minutes

Story: Camp Crystal Lake, 1958. While a group of summer camp counsellors unwind singing campfire songs, two of their number break off and go to an outhouse to make out. Disturbed by an unseen intruder they are both murdered.

Friday June 13th. The Present.

Despite ominous warnings, Steve Christy and his helpers (studious ex-girlfriend Alice, joker Ned, randy couple Jack and Marcie and impetuous Brenda) are busy reopening Camp Crystal Lake. The last counsellor, Annie, has not arrived by the time Steve drives off to pick up more supplies, because she is still hitch-hiking to the camp. Accepting a lift from an unseen driver, she is soon murdered.

Back at the site, the others are unaware that they are being watched from the woods.

Night begins to fall, Ned wanders off on his own and thinks he sees someone in the boathouse... The impending storm breaks and Marcie and Jack retire to one of the bunkhouses. They have sex, unaware that Ned's corpse is on the bunk above them. Afterwards, when Marcie goes to the toilet, Jack is murdered by someone under the bed. Convinced that she has been followed, Marcie checks the shower stalls only to find the killer, who puts an axe through her head. After spending the evening smoking dope, drinking beer and playing strip Monopoly, Brenda goes to her cabin, leaving Alice (who never even lost her blouse) and Bill to tidy up. She is drawn back out by a child's voice calling for help. Someone meets her at the archery range and her scream is drowned out by the thunder. Bill and Alice go out looking for the others only to find a bloodied axe in Brenda's bed and no one around. They also find the phones and the van have been disabled.

On his return to the camp, Steve seems to recognise his killer.

Bill goes to fix the generator and Alice drifts off to sleep, waking later to go in search of the others. Finding Bill pinned to a door with arrows, she barricades herself in the main cabin until Brenda's corpse is thrown through the window. Now completely panicked, she races to greet a jeep. The driver, Mrs Voorhees, 'an old friend of the Christys,' seems aghast at what she finds. But then she explains that she used to be the cook at the camp and was working the day that her son, Jason, drowned due to being left unsupervised by the counsellors. Friday The 13th is his birthday. Alice manages to brain her with a poker as Mrs Voorhees' personality blurs with Jason's (who urges Alice's murder) and, discovering various corpses en route, a desperate chase ensues ending when Alice finally decapitates her attacker with a machete.

Awakening in a small boat on the lake, Alice hears the police cars arriving, and is pulled overboard by Jason's vengeful corpse.

Background: Sean S Cunningham started in the film industry making soft-core porn in the early 70s after producing theatre in New York. His movie career was given a major boost when he was hired to produce the film that also made Wes Craven's name: *Last House On The Left* (1972). Cunningham's career was in the doldrums after that, directing cheap reworkings of Michael Richie's *The Bad News Bears* (1976): *Here Come The Tigers* (1978) and *Manny's Orphans* (1979). He cast around for a roller-coaster shocker that would put him into the big time and came up with *Friday The 13th*. Made on the cheap using friends and locations in his home state of Connecticut, the film was picked up for distribution by Paramount and was thus given the kind of advertising campaign that a small independent film could only dream of. However, despite the presence of the big league, the campaign itself was still very much in style of independent distributors such as Hallmark, who distributed *Last House* with the now immortal tag-line 'Keep telling yourself it's only a movie... only a movie... only a movie,' except more brutal. The poster depicted a shadowy outline carrying a knife. Inside the outline was a picture of some teenagers in the woods. 'They are doomed,' ran the slogan. The movie trailer was even more explicit, exaggerating the body count - there are thirteen victims in the trailer but only ten in the movie, most of whose deaths are off-screen, but that's advertising. The film was a huge success, netting over seventeen million dollars in the US alone convincing film companies, both major and independent, that slasher movies were the way to make a fast killing at the box office.

Despite *Friday The 13th*'s faults (and there are many), it does exactly what it says on the tin. A bog-standard scary movie with splashy effects, cheap shocks and a roller-coaster feel to the whole proceedings. Stealing from so many movies, it comes as no real surprise that the killer in all its sequels is a regenerated corpse. Taking *Halloween*'s prowling camera and placing it à la *Peeping Tom* so that the audience is put in the killing seat, Harry Manfredini's score also steals Bernard Herrmann's kill-kill-kill string riff from *Psycho*'s shower scene (and would continue to utilise it through the rest of the series). Even the shock ending is lifted wholesale from *Carrie* (1976). As with many slasher movies, the storyline is constructed along the lines of Agatha Christie's *Ten Little Indians* but despite brief attempts to mislead us as to who the killer might be (Bill's usefulness with a machete, Steve driving a similar jeep to the one that picks up Annie) it becomes clear that no one initially introduced is the killer, because they're virtually all dead by the third reel. In effect, Tom Savini's special effects become the star as well as the film's raison d'être simply because, unlike the doomed teens in *Texas Chainsaw Massacre* or *Halloween*, no character is developed enough for us to really care about them.

It is however, the film that cemented the slasher conventions of girls going out in the pouring rain, in the dark, on their own, in their underwear (both Brenda and Marcie do it), and the fact that you must <u>never</u> stand in front of a window.

Final girl Alice is sketched in with the briefest of strokes but still the depth afforded her is unfathomable in comparison with the others at the campsite, and so when she proves to be the last on her feet it comes as no great surprise. She loses no clothes during strip Monopoly, she doesn't go out in the woods in her underwear, she knows how to repair the generator, is artistic and worries about the others - above all, she has no sex during the length of the film. You figure it out.

Verdict: 3/5

After *Friday The 13th*'s success, Cunningham removed himself from the ongoing series until *Jason Goes To Hell - The Final Friday* (1993), but returned to the horror genre with the lighter in tone *House* series.

5. Slasher Heydays

'It happened once, it happened twice.
Cancel the dance or it'll happen thrice.'

- My Bloody Valentine

Between 1980 and 1982 you could hardly go near a cinema or enter a video store without some knife-wielding psychopath lurking just off-screen. Below are just a few examples of the various themes, settings and conventions that the slasher movie employed during this boom period.

Halloween 2 (1981)

Cast: Jamie Lee Curtis (Laurie Strode), Donald Pleasence (Loomis), Charles Cyphers (Leigh Brackett), Lance Guest (Jimmy), Pamela Susan Shoop (Karen), Nancy Stephens (Marion), Ford Rainey (Dr Mixter), Dick Warlock (The Shape/Michael Myers)

Crew: Director Rick Rosenthal, Producers/Writers John Carpenter & Debra Hill, Cinematography Dean Cundey, Music John Carpenter & Alan Howarth, Editors Mark Goldblatt & Skip Schoolnik, Production Designer Michael Riva, Special Effects Larry Cavanaugh, 92 minutes

Story: Following on from the first *Halloween*, Laurie is taken to Haddonfield General Hospital. Loomis continues his hunt for Michael Myers, and is briefly stalled when it appears that Michael has been incinerated in a car accident. However, the killings continue and it is revealed that Michael is trying to kill Laurie because she is his sister, adopted by another family shortly after Michael killed Judith. After Michael kills most of the hospital staff in pursuit of Laurie, she is saved by Loomis, who destroys Michael but is blown up in the process.

Background: An unnecessary sequel (aren't they all?) which takes place in the emptiest hospital ever committed to celluloid. The only patient (apart from a few babies) appears to be Laurie. The simplicity of the first *Halloween* was that no explanation was needed. It was assumed that Michael saw his sister in Laurie after spotting her walking to school with Tommy (a boy about the same age as he had been when he killed Judith), so the surprise family revelation (something that also would be played out at some point or other in *A Nightmare On Elm Street* and *Friday The 13th* sequels) smacks of desperation. John Carpenter wrote the script with Debra Hill and he is also responsible for the increased gore quota in this sequel, reshooting sequences after director Rosenthal had finished. As ever, the theme music and Dean Cundey's prowling camerawork add an air of menace to the proceedings but it's pretty standard stuff in comparison to the original. Editing duties were performed by Mark Goldblatt who went on to work with James Cameron, and Skip Schoolnik who occasionally directs episodes of *Buffy The Vampire Slayer*.

After this sequel Michael Myers retired for a few years. *Halloween III - Season Of The Witch*, was an attempt to move the series away from the slasher genre and into more original horror themes. It was written by *Quatermass* creator Nigel Kneale who withdrew his credit in protest at script changes.

Verdict: 3/5

Here are some more medical/hospital-based slashers which feature a similar lack of patients: *Phobia* (1980), directed by John Huston, starred Paul Michael Glaser as a psychotherapist treating his patients by confronting them with their phobias, the same method by which a serial killer is disposing of them; the misogynistic *Visiting Hours* (1981) where woman-in-peril Lee Grant is pursued by mother-abused psychopath Michael Ironside; and *X-Ray* (1982, aka *Hospital Massacre, Be My Valentine Or Else!*) had ex-*Playboy* centrefold Barbi Benton turning up for a routine examination and being terrorised by a spurned childhood sweetheart. The later *Dr Giggles* (1993), which starred Larry Drake as the eponymous killer, continued the now-standard humorous punchline per victim as perfected by Freddy Krueger.

Prom Night (1980)

Cast: Leslie Nielsen (Principal Hammond), Jamie Lee Curtis (Kim), Casey Stevens (Nick), Eddie Benton (Wendy), Michael Tough (Alex), Robert Silverman (Sykes), David Mucci (Lou), Marybeth Rubens (Kelly), George Touliatos (Lt McBride), Jeff Wincott (Drew), Joy Thompson (Jude), Sheldon Rybowski (Slick), Antoinette Bower (Mrs Hammond)

Crew: Director Paul Lynch, Producer Peter Simpson, Writers William Gray & Robert Guza Jr, Cinematography Robert New, Music Carl Zittrer & Paul Zaza, Editor Brian Ravok, Art Director Reuben Freed, Special Effects Al Cotter & Warren Keillor, 95 minutes

Story: On the sixth anniversary of their sister Robin's death, Kim and Alex Hammond prepare for their senior prom. Believed the victim of the psychotic Leonard Murch, Robin's death was actually an accident, caused by four older children: Wendy, Nick, Kelly and Jude. The three girls receive threatening phone calls just after Murch escapes from an asylum, taking a nurse hostage. During the school day, Wendy, jealous at Nick's affections for Kim forms an alliance with hardcase Lou to exact her revenge. After finding the body of Murch's hostage killed with a glass shard at the site of Robin's death, Lieutenant McBride stakes out the school, convinced the maniac is out for revenge. That night, while prom king and queen Kim and Nick prepare for their duties Kelly, left alone, is murdered with a piece of glass. Jude and her new lover Slick make out and are killed shortly afterwards. The killer, armed with an axe, stalks and kills Wendy. Hearing of Murch's capture McBride leaves the premises. As Nick, preparing for the crowning ceremony, is stalked by the killer, Lou knocks him unconscious and takes his place on the catwalk, getting decapitated instead of Nick. In the ensuing panic, Kim strikes the killer who is revealed to be Alex, avenging Robin's death.

Background: The best of the 80s high-school slashers, *Prom Night* benefits from decent performances and an eventful plot that tries to keep its audience guessing the murderer's identity. Benton and Mucci seem to have been modelled on Nancy Allen and John Travolta's characters in *Carrie*, but both chew the scenery in a suitably villainous fashion and gain a satisfactory come-uppance. Director Lynch, who later turned in the dreadful *Humungous* (1981), another kids-in-the-woods-menaced-by-deformed-maniac farrago, manages to keep the tension high and the plot moving, particularly in the scene where Curtis freaks out at the sounds of broken glass being swept up and in the well-choreographed finale. While Cronenberg regular Silverman has little to do other than leer and play drunk, Leslie Nielsen's disco dancing proves that humour was where his talents lay.

Verdict: 4/5

Various slashers used high school and campus settings to varying degrees of effectiveness. *Terror Eyes* (1980, aka *Night School*), directed by *Chitty Chitty Bang Bang's* Ken Hughes, had female students being decapitated by the jealous girlfriend (Rachel Ward) of a randy academic (Drew Snyder) and featured another severed head in the toilet scene. *Graduation Day* (1981) had a killer avenging the death of the star of the high school's track team, whereas the murderer in *Final Exam* (1981) needed no reasons for killing people, he just did it. *The Dorm That Dripped Blood* (1982, aka *Pranks*), did away with the final girl so that the class geek/killer escaped and *House Of Sorority Row* (1982, aka *House Of Evil*) was directed by Brian De Palma protégé Mark Rosman who appeared to have learned everything he knew from the *Co-Ed Frenzy* slasher scene in *Blow Out* (1981). Two other, better examples are *Terror Train* and *Hell Night*.

Terror Train (1980)

Cast: Ben Johnson (Charlie), Jamie Lee Curtis (Alana), Hart Bochner (Doc), Sandee Currie (Mitchy), Timothy Webber (Mo), Derek MacKinnon (Kenny Hampson), David Copperfield (Magician), Anthony Sherwood (Jackson), Jay Boushel (Pet), DD Winters (Merry), Greg Swanson (Class President), Howard Busgang (Ed)

Crew: Director Roger Spottiswoode, Producer Harold Greenberg, Writer T Y Drake, Music John Mills-Cockell, Cinematography John Alcott, Editor Anne Henderson, Production Designer Glenn Bydwell, Special Make-Up Effects Alan Friedman, 97 minutes

Story: Four years after pledge Kenny Hampson has been hospitalised as a result of a fraternity prank, the graduating members of a medical college throw a fancy dress party on a train, organised by the prank's ringleaders, Doc and Mo. On board people are murdered by a killer who switches disguises each time he claims a victim. Both Charlie the conductor and Mo's girlfriend, Alana, sense that something is wrong. Their suspicions are confirmed when Mitchy, Alana's best friend, is discovered dead. Believing that Kenny is the killer, Alana suspects that the hired magician is, in fact, Kenny. Mo is killed during part of the magician's act and the engineer disappears. The conductor stops the train and forces everyone to dismount and unmask but Doc has hidden on the train. The conductor locks everyone in the carriage away from the magician and places Alana under the ticket inspector's protection. Alana is attacked by the killer, only to find that it is Kenny, who has been working as the magician's assistant. In a final struggle, the conductor reappears and they throw Kenny from the train.

Background: The combined pedigrees of Alcott (Stanley Kubrick's cinematographer) and Spottiswoode (Sam Peckinpah's editor) suggest that *Terror Train* shouldn't fail to be a superior slasher but it follows the formula a little too faithfully (the hazing prank gone awry, oversexed teens, vengeance wreaked) to allow for any distinctiveness. That said, Alcott films the endless dim corridors as true places of horror and the film yields several extremely tense moments, most notably when class cad Doc locks Alana out of his carriage only to realise that he's locked himself in with the killer. Veteran western actor Ben Johnson turns in a fine performance as the authoritative conductor, bemoaning the end of the train as a viable form of transport and Jamie Lee Curtis adds another intelligent final girl to her gallery of screaming, resourceful heroines. The neat twist of hiding the murderer in plain view (albeit in drag) merely makes one wonder how anyone could think that someone could change so dramatically in four years that they would suddenly look like David Copperfield.

Verdict: 3/5

Hell Night (1981)

Cast: Linda Blair (Marti), Vincent Van Patten (Seth), Kevin Brophy (Peter), Suki Goodwin (Denise), Jenny Neumann (May), Jimmy Sturtevant (Scott), Peter Barton (Jeff)

Crew: Director Tom De Simone, Producers Irwin Yablans & Bruce Cohn Curtis, Writer Randolph Feldman, Cinematography Mac Ahlberg, Music Dan Wyman, Editor Tony Di Marco, Art Director Steven C Legler, 102 minutes

Story: For their fraternity/sorority initiations, college freshmen Marti, Jeff, Seth and Denise agree to spend a night in Garth Manor where, twelve years previously, Raymond Garth murdered his wife and three of his monstrous brood before committing suicide. The event was witnessed by the fourth child, Andrew, who is alleged to still live in the house. The freshmen pair off, and quickly realise that seniors May, Scott and Peter have rigged the house with spook devices which the couples disable. However, something is also quick to disable May, Scott and Peter before abducting Denise after she has slept with Seth. Awaking to find May's severed head beside him, Seth rouses Jeff and Marti and they help him to climb over the locked gates to fetch help. The local police think Seth's pleas for help are a collegiate prank and he is reduced to stealing a shotgun from the police station. Marti and Jeff discover a basement littered with corpses. Seth returns only to be set upon, manages to shoot and kill his attacker, but is killed himself by a second monstrous figure. Jeff is also murdered, but Marti escapes after finding the gate keys on Peter's corpse. As she tries to drive away, the monster grabs at her from the car roof but is killed outright when Marti drives at the gate, ramming it onto the spikes.

Background: Well-mounted no-frills university slasher with fine performances all round. Despite the odd plot hole (did no one ever remove the original bodies from the crime scene twelve years ago and who is Seth's attacker?), ex-porno director De Simone lets the tension and the bodies mount at a steady pace and the freshmen characters are, for once, allowed a modicum of intelligence. Photography by Ahlberg (another ex-porno director, who later worked on *The Brady Bunch Movie*) is atmospheric particularly in the exterior sequences. Placing the characters in period fancy dress lends the tale an air of Brothers Grimm while Blair (who is famous for some film or other) makes a splendid final girl, proudly telling Jeff of her childhood with her car-mechanic dad as a prelude to the finale where she rapidly fixes the motor of the car that will take her to safety.

Verdict: 4/5

My Bloody Valentine (1981)

Cast: Paul Kelman (TJ), Lori Hallier (Sarah), Neil Affleck (Axel), Don Francks (Chief Newby), Keith Knight (Hollis), Alf Humphreys (Howard), Cynthia Dale (Patty), Terry Waterland (Harriet), Patricia Hamilton (Mabel), Larry Reynolds (Mayor Hanniger), Jack Van Evera (Happy), Peter Cowper (Harry Warden)

Crew: Director George Mihalka, Producers Andre Link & John Dunning & Stephen Miller, Writer John Beaird, Cinematography Rodney Gibbons, Music Paul Zaza, Editor Jean Lafleur, Art Director Penny Hadfield, Special Make-Up Effects Tom Burman & Ken Diaz & Tom Hoerber, 91 minutes

Story: It is twenty-one years after a cave-in on Valentine's Day at the Hanniger mine which resulted in the deaths of five miners and the rescue of Harry Warden, insane after resorting to cannibalism for his survival. The town of Valentine Bluffs is set to hold its first Valentine's Day ball since Harry killed the two supervisors whose attendance at the ball caused the miners' deaths. A heart-shaped chocolate box delivered to the mayor is revealed to contain a human heart and Harry Warden is believed to have returned. Meanwhile, emotions are high at the mine - TJ Hanniger has returned to town and finds his old flame Sarah has taken up with his rival, Axel. When the ball's organiser is murdered, the mayor halts the festivities to appease the vengeful Harry, but the miners hold a secret Valentine party at the mine and the killings continue. When the deaths are discovered, TJ and Axel race to save a group of party-goers, including Sarah, who are touring the mine. As the dwindling party try to escape, they discover that Axel, traumatised as a child after witnessing Harry kill his father, is the murderer. TJ and Sarah are saved and a cave-in buries Axel. They watch in horror as he severs his trapped arm and staggers into the mine vowing further revenge.

Background: This grim little slasher is one of the few that features characters in lives outside of academia. But while they might work hard, they also play hard, which allows for plentiful scenes of drinking, making out and foolish behaviour. While you might not expect social realism, the movie does not explore the possibly more fertile ground of industrial small-town life in favour of rhubarbing locals and a few mumbled lines about TJ's failure in New York. Director Mihalka manages a few atmospheric scenes, including the climax and, for once, the past tragedy is told in flashback rather than as a pre-credits sequence. Despite these and the genuinely creepy figure of the deranged miner in full garb, the plot contrivances and wooden acting effectively scupper the movie.

Verdict: 2/5

One of a series of anniversary slashers, running on from *Halloween* and *Friday The 13th*, these usually involved some dreadful deed that had occurred on a specific date. Once a suitable period had elapsed, the anniversary of the occurrence would either spark revenge from the original maniac, or someone pretending to be them. Other entries include: *Happy Birthday To Me* (1980) directed by J Lee Thompson, starred *Little House On The Prairie*'s Melissa Sue Anderson as the main target (and suspect) in a series of slayings that climaxes in a gruesome birthday party attended by all the corpses; *New Year's Evil* (1980) in which an ultra-punctual maniac attempts to claim a victim each time midnight strikes in the time zones across the US; *The Prowler* (1981, aka *Rosemary's Killer*) has a small town holding its first graduation ball in 35 years, only to spark off a series of killings by a vengeful GI; and *Don't Open Till Christmas* (1984) and *Silent Night Deadly Night* (1984) which both featured Santa-slashing and Santa-psychos, the latter movie spawning four sequels.

Friday The 13th Part 2 (1981)

Cast: Amy Steel (Ginny), John Furey (Paul), Adrienne King (Alice), Kirsten Baker (Terry), Stu Charno (Ted), Warrington Gillette (Jason), Walt Gorney (Crazy Ralph), Marta Kober (Sandra), Tom McBride (Mark), Bill Randolph (Jeff), Lauren-Marie Taylor (Vickie), Russell Todd (Scott), Betsy Palmer (Mrs Voorhees)

Crew: Director/Producer Steve Miner, Writer Ron Kurz, Associate Producer Frank Mancuso Jr, Cinematography Peter Stein, Music Harry Manfredini, Editor Susan E Cunningham, Production Designer Virginia Field, Special Make-Up Effects Carl Fullerton & David Smith & John Caglione Jr, 87 minutes

Story: Still recovering from the trauma of the murders at Camp Crystal Lake, Alice finds Mrs Voorhees' mummified head in her fridge just before an intruder kills her with an ice pick.

Five years later a group of counsellors converge at the newly-opened Camp Counsellor Training Center run by Paul and his sometime paramour assistant, child psychology major Ginny. They are already being watched. Paul scotches rumours about Jason still being alive in the woods to no avail. Before their real training the group go to a local bar for the evening, leaving six counsellors. By the time Ginny and Paul arrive back, they have all been murdered. With Paul knocked out by the masked assailant, Ginny runs, ending up at Jason's shack. Discovering a shrine to his mother including her mummified head, she plays the mother, satisfied with her son's performance and manages to 'kill' him with a machete.

Background: Like many slashers of the period, *Friday The 13th Part 2* sustained cuts for UK distribution but, more notably, it was the first slasher to encounter problems at the Motion Picture Association of America (MPAA), whose concerns over the scene where a couple are speared during sex, led to the recommendation that the film receive an X rating - a rating normally reserved for hard-core porn and thus certain death for any film hoping to gain major distribution. Curiously, the make-up effects people were the most upset by this verdict, viewing it as censoring their artistry. Paramount trimmed the scene, the film gained the more acceptable R rating and Paramount took over $10 million at the US box office alone.

Paramount's attitude in presenting and marketing this hasty follow-up was questionable. The movie's poster tagline was 'The body count continues' and some of the plot machinations in this sequel require such a profound suspension of disbelief that you can hear the ropes creaking under the weight. However, *Friday The 13th Part 2* is efficiently directed and well paced. If one can get past the notion of Jason going from drowned ten-year-old to lumbering backwoods maniac in five years (a prodigious amount of hormone-spurts by any account), then the rest of the film unfolds in slasher-blueprint fashion, with the slow build-up to the slaughter kept tense by Miner's direction. The killing of Alice at the start is callous but logical - she has faced her monster in the form of Mrs Voorhees. Ginny's character is immediately presented as the obvious final girl - level-headed, relatively abstemious and intelligent. One small point, other than Jason's close resemblance to John Hurt in *The Elephant Man*, the most curious thing about *Friday The 13th Part 2* is that it contains the genuinely bizarre and inexplicable pre-credits sequence of Jason taking Alice's kettle off the boil after he has killed her.

Verdict: 3/5

As well as *The Burning* (see below), the campsite slasher movie proved particularly popular (presumably because little set construction was required), and countless teens were butchered in the primeval woods in films such as: *Just Before Dawn* (1980) in which the heroine kills the villain by choking him with her arm; *Campsite Massacre* (1981) with Rachel Ward and Daryl Hannah among those being stalked; *Madman* (1982) was a no-frills *Friday The 13th* copy; and *Sleepaway Camp* (1983), which replayed the *Homicidal* twist and spawned two equally poor sequels, was practically played for laughs. Later, Ruggero Deodato would provide *Camping Del Terrore* (1986, aka *Body Count*), which featured slashers from other movies, David Hess, Mimsy Farmer and John Steiner, in non-slasher roles, leaving the carnage to the teenagers.

The Burning (1980)

Cast: Brian Matthews (Tod), Leah Ayres (Michelle), Brian Backer (Alfred), Larry Joshua (Glazer), Jason Alexander (Dave), Ned Eisenberg (Eddy), Carrick Glenn (Sally), Carolyn Houlihan (Karen), Fisher Stevens (Woodstock), Lou David (Cropsy)

Crew: Director Tony Maylam, Producer Harvey Weinstein, Story Weinstein & Maylam & Brad Grey, Screenplay Peter Lawrence & Bob Weinstein, Cinematography Harvey Harrison, Music Rick Wakeman, Editor Jack Sholder, Art Director Peter Politanoff, Special Make-Up Effects Tom Savini, 91 minutes

Story: Five years after a prank that results in Camp Blackfoot's sadistic handyman Cropsy being burned alive (the rarity of a prank going humorously right in a slasher film is a cause for celebration), a new campsite welcomes its campers, only for many of them to be picked off and slaughtered during a trip upriver by a vengeful Cropsy and his garden shears. Eventually he is destroyed by two of the campers.

Background: The Burning is one of many campsite mayhem movies made on the back of *Friday The 13th*. It was the Weinstein brothers' shot at turning their fledgling distribution company Miramax (set up in 1979) over to production and the resulting revenues couldn't have hurt. In place of any genuine suspense, there is a lengthy, lethargic build-up to the murders while campers bully, screw and play lame jokes on each other, wander through darkened woods while being stalked by a subjective camera, and drink lots of beer. Tom Savini's gory effects fill in the rest along with lots of rowing scenes.

The Burning differs from many slashers of the era in that the final girl is a boy, Alfred who, after many of the terrified campers have been rowed to safety by a female counsellor, is hunted down by Cropsy but ends up going to the rescue of Tod (one of the ringleaders of the prank that got Cropsy horribly burned in the first place). Also, Alfred isn't a particularly sympathetic or savoury character, being whiny, generally cowardly and voyeuristic, spying on at least two couples who happen to be frolicking semi-naked while their colleagues are disappearing left, right and centre (giving a new resonance to the term 'unsafe sex'). However, it could be argued that, if nothing else, Harvey Weinstein knows teenage boys, particularly the sort that would shell out good money to see this epic and therefore gives them a 'hero' that they can identify with. In every other respect the film is shamefully derivative which, as with many of the boom-era slashers, gives it what power it does have - the idiot factor is upped and the audience sighs with relief, knowing that they would never be so dumb as to make out in the middle of a deserted forest and that anyone who does so is asking for it. The only other noticeable departure from the blueprint is that when Alfred witnesses a murder and goes to fetch help the helper returns with him and the body is still there - a surprisingly refreshing twist although it was probably only so Savini's handiwork (a severed head) could be shown for a second time.

Verdict: 1/5

He Knows You're Alone (1980)

Cast: Don Scardino (Marvin), Caitlin O'Heaney (Amy), Elizabeth Kemp (Nancy), Lewis Arlt (Len Gamble), Patsy Pease (Joyce), James Rebhorn (Professor), Tom Hanks (Elliott), Dana Barron (Diana), Tom Rolfing (Killer), James Carroll (Phil), Joseph Leon (Ralph)

Crew: Director Armand Mastroianni, Producer George Manasse, Writer Scott Parker, Cinematography Gerald Feil, Music Mark & Alexander Peskanov, Editor George T Norris, Art Director Susan Kaufman, Special Make-Up Effects Taso N Stavrakis, 94 minutes

Story: Detective Gamble's fiancée is murdered by her ex-boyfriend. Gamble, convinced that a bride-to-be is the next victim, tracks the killer to a wedding dressmaker whose latest customer, Amy, is having doubts about her forthcoming marriage to Phil, now away on a bachelor party weekend. The killer stalks Amy and her friends, whilst she is reunited with her ex, Marvin, a morgue attendant. After several of her friends are killed, the maniac pursues Amy to the morgue where Marvin struggles with him and is knocked unconscious. Gamble shoots the killer but he rises again and fatally stabs the policeman. In a final chase, Amy traps the killer as the police arrive. On her wedding day, Amy has decided to marry Marvin, but Phil shows up with murder in mind...

Background: Opening with a scene taken from the urban legend of the couple menaced in Lovers Lane by a maniac, the camera pulls back to reveal we are watching a film in a cinema with the first victim and her friend. It's the only surprise in store in this leaden women-in-peril slasher half-heartedly yoked to a police procedural. Containing the outright prizewinner for the score most derivative of the theme from *Halloween*, *He Knows You're Alone* partly redeems itself at the climax, generating mild suspense and symbolism as Amy is chased down the long, long, long tunnel from the morgue to the hospital, but a lack of satisfactory outcome (a slasher-movie villain getting arrested?) and the cheap twist ending swiftly dissipate its effect. Mastroianni continued to turn in uninteresting horror movies (*The Supernaturals* (1986), *Cameron's Closet* (1988)) before graduating to making the sort of TV movie thrillers usually scheduled for late-night midweek viewing. Tom Hanks survived the movie in more ways than one.

Verdict: 1/5

While the slasher movie cannot lay claim to exclusive rights to the woman-in-peril theme (it being a constant motif throughout the horror genre), it produced both hugely misogynist exploitation pictures such as *Maniac* (1980), *Don't Go In The House* (1980) and Lucio Fulci's *The New York Ripper* (1981) as well as the more interesting *Slumber Party Massacre* (1982) which was directed by Amy Jones and written by Rita Mae Brown, the author of *Rubyfruit Jungle*. While its plot consisted of the usual slasher malarkey of a bunch of under-dressed teenage girls being tormented and killed by a drill-wielding maniac, the climax consisted of the remaining girls symbolically snapping the end off of his drill-bit before doing him in. A later effort, *Out Of The Dark* (1988), had a psychopathic clown killing girls working for a phone-sex company and managed to waste the combined talents of Geoffrey Lewis, Paul Bartel, Karen Black, Bud Cort, Tracey Walter and Divine - no mean feat.

The Funhouse (1981)

Cast: Elizabeth Berridge (Amy), Cooper Huckabee (Buzz), Miles Chapin (Richie), Largo Woodruff (Liz), Sylvia Miles (Madame Zena), William Finley (Marco The Magnificent), Kevin Conway (The Barker), Wayne Doba (The Monster), Shawn Carson (Joey Harper)

Crew: Director Tobe Hooper, Producers Derek Power & Steven Bernhardt, Writer Larry Block, Cinematography Andrew Laszlo, Music John Beal, Editor Jack Hofstra, Production Designer Morton Rabinowitz, Special Make-Up Effects Rick Baker & Craig Reardon, 96 minutes

Story: Electing to spend the night in a carnival funhouse, two teenage couples (Amy and Buzz, Richie and Liz) witness a sexual assignation between fortune-teller Madame Zena and one of the carnival staff who remains masked. Zena taunts him and he kills her. Investigating the scene of the crime, Richie unwisely steals from a cash box. When the fairground barker finds the box empty, he accuses the masked man. During an argument the masked man is revealed to be the barker's son - his mask slips showing his hideously deformed face. The barker discovers the couples and they are pursued through the funhouse by him and his murderous son. Richie and Liz are murdered and a bloody fight between Buzz and the barker kills them both. When Amy is cornered in the funhouse engine room by the monster, she shoves him into the machinery and he is crushed to death.

Background: It opens with an entertaining parody of both *Psycho* and *Halloween* (Amy is menaced in the shower by a knife-wielding figure disguised as a clown, the figure is revealed to be her little brother, the knife made of rubber). Released in the UK in a double bill with *My Bloody Valentine*, *The Funhouse* was to be Hooper's last film of major interest. As with *The Texas Chainsaw Massacre,* Hooper's preoccupations remain the same: the monstrous family with the monster both abused and loved by his father. An exploration of the nature of the monster, here human, but monstrously disfigured, he spends his days disguised as Frankenstein's monster, a figure sanitised by absorption into the cultural mainstream. Again, the mix of black comedy and outright horror is effective and, although the film carries far less power than *The Texas Chainsaw Massacre*, it is well above average fare. Berridge, who seems to have been cast for her striking resemblance to Jessica Harper circa *Suspiria* (1976), turns in an excellent performance, no less so than in the film's bleakest sequence which echoes *The Incredible Shrinking Man* (1955). In this scene, frustratingly separated from the outside world by a huge air-conditioning fan, she sees her parents beyond the whirling blades, summoned to collect her errant brother Joey, who has secretly followed her to the carnival. Joey's fearful loyalty to her keeps her presence a secret, her screams for help are blown straight back at her.

Verdict: 4/5

6. New Blood And More Blood

"I've seen enough horror movies to know any weirdo wearing a mask is never friendly"

- Friday The 13th Part VI

'Speaking of people who look like scrambled eggs, *Friday The 13th Part 5: A New Beginning* is the best Spam-in-a-cabin flick since *Friday The 13th Part 2*. I don't wanna put down *3* and *4*, but let's face it, after fifty-two kids die in the same cabin, it's time to try something new. They got a new cabin.'

- Joe-Bob Briggs

Friday The 13th - The Body Count Drags On

The production of slasher movies reduced quite dramatically after 1982 but, like their killers, they wouldn't stay dead. The *Friday The 13th* franchise continued to produce new chapters at the pace of nearly one a year until 1989. The popularity of the series amongst gore-hungry teens, despite diminishing box office returns on each episode, kept it running long after all permutations had run out and shameless genre pillaging had taken over. Obviously the first two parts weren't exactly free of theft but they contained a certain amount of power and tension in their portrayal of violent deaths and the struggles to overcome vicious killers that balanced out the plagiarism. However, once the series had settled on Jason, the bulky permanently-enraged guardian of the backwoods, the formula became static as well.

Friday The 13th Part 3 (1983) was filmed in 3-D during a revival of the format but released flat on video. This is the one where Jason gets his trademark hockey mask. Following on from events in Part 2, Jason kills another bunch of dumb teens and pokes lots of pointy weapons out of the screen. Its high (and low) point comes when Final Girl Chris's boyfriend has his head squeezed until his eyeball flies out at the audience. Chris kills Jason with an axe but the resurrected corpse of Mrs Voorhees gets her - oh dear. Part 3 was limply directed by Steve Miner who, after moving on to more family-oriented fare such as *Forever Young* (1992), would return to the slasher with *Halloween H20* (1998). *Verdict: 2/5*

Friday The 13th - The Final Chapter (1984) fooled no one, except maybe the character who stands in a darkened kitchen and asks 'Where's the corkscrew?' Jason revives in the morgue, kills some very irritating teens and is finally dispatched by twelve-year-old Tommy Jarvis (Corey

Feldman, the 80s answer to Macauley Culkin). Director Joseph Zito also made anniversary slasher *Rosemary's Killer* (1981, aka *The Prowler*). *Verdict:* 2/5

Friday The 13th - A New Beginning (1985, director Danny Steinmann) appears to have been written by ex -*Scooby-Doo* scripters. Set in a halfway house for disturbed teens, it looks like Jason is back when everyone starts getting slaughtered. But who's that bit-part actor bugging out his eyes? Could *he* be the killer disguised as Jason? He would've gotten away with it too, if it hadn't been for that meddling Tommy Jarvis. Includes the most pointless reverse zoom ever committed to celluloid. *Verdict:* 1/5

Jason Lives - Friday The 13th Part VI (1986) showed how the series was now being influenced by *A Nightmare On Elm Street*, with Jason resurrected as a zombie, thanks to a timely lightning bolt. Director Tom McLoughlin tries to inject some humour but with 17 victims to pack into one movie it's not easy. Having accidentally brought Jason back in the first place, Tommy Jarvis finally plants him at the bottom of Crystal Lake. *Verdict:* 1/5

Friday The 13th Part VII - The New Blood (1988). It's *Carrie* vs. Jason as telekinetic Tina, regretting the fact that she drowned her abusive father in Crystal Lake, wishes him back and resurrects old hockey-mask-face instead. Carnage ensues until Tina finally rouses dad, who pulls Jason back down into the watery depths. Don't the authorities ever drag these places? Directed by special effects man John Carl Buechler, this instalment has all the subtlety his initials suggest. *Verdict:* 1/5

Friday The 13th Part VIII - Jason Takes Manhattan (1989, director Rob Hedden). Virtually gore-free *Love Boat* episode as Jason, awoken by a severed power cable, climbs aboard the good ship Lazarus (ho-ho) and slaughters various graduating party-goers. Climaxes in a kind of MTV/Abel Ferrara New York (actually Toronto) where Jason, killed by toxic sludge, reverts to the form of a small boy, suggesting that he's been a ghost all along, rather than a zombie, or something. *Verdict:* 0/5

Are You Ready For Freddy?

As Paramount continued bleeding the *Friday The 13th* format drier than one of Jason's victims, 1985 saw the release of a film that would not only reinvigorate the genre but would pave the way for its acceptance by mainstream studios and audiences.

Having worked on ill-fated projects *Swamp Thing* (1981) and *The Hills Have Eyes 2* (1984), director Wes Craven was due for a break. *A Nightmare On Elm Street* had been his long-cherished project and the script had been circulating in Hollywood for at least three years before New Line head Robert Shaye finally secured the necessary finance. Virtually broke by the time the film came to shoot, Craven signed away the rights to New Line and it was this loss of control that led to half-witted sequels and a slow dilution of Krueger's primal nastiness, tainting the memory of the original. It would, however, establish New Line as an exploitation force and, more than *Scream* (1997), it is for *A Nightmare On Elm Street* that Craven will be best remembered.

A Nightmare On Elm Street (1984)

Cast: John Saxon (Lt Thompson), Ronee Blakley (Marge Thompson), Heather Langenkamp (Nancy Thompson), Amanda Wyss (Tina Gray), Nick Corri (Rod Lane), Johnny Depp (Glen Lantz), Charles Fleischer (Dr King), Joseph Whipp (Sgt Parker), Lin Shaye (Teacher), Robert Englund (Fred Krueger)

Crew: Director/Writer Wes Craven, Producer Robert Shaye, Cinematography Jacques Haitkin, Editor Rick Shaine, Music Charles Bernstein, Production Designer Greg Fonseca, Mechanical Special Effects Jim Doyle, Theatrical Engines & Special Make-Up Effects David Miller, 91 minutes

Story: The teenagers of Elm Street, Nancy, Rod, Glen and Tina are having deadly nightmares. All their dreams feature the same darkened boiler room through which they are stalked by a blade-fingered demon wearing a battered hat and a striped jersey. While boyfriend Rod watches Tina as she sleeps, she is butchered by an unseen assailant. Lt Thompson, Nancy's father, arrests Rod for Tina's murder and despite Nancy's growing realisation that the demon in the nightmares can physically harm them in the real world, she and Glen are too late to save Rod. Later, Nancy discovers that it may be possible to pull their assailant into the real world having awoken holding its hat. A label inside the hat reads 'Fred Krueger.' Confronted by that name, Nancy's mother confesses that Fred Krueger was a child murderer who was burned alive as an act of revenge by the Elm Street parents but she refuses to accept his continued existence. After witnessing Glen's murder, Nancy finally pulls Krueger out into the real world and, while her booby traps help to slow him down, it is her denial of his existence that stops him. However...

Background: Here, at last, Craven's intelligence and love of surrealism shine through. In *Halloween*, Michael Myers might be referred to as 'the boogeyman' but Krueger, in terms of his abilities, the folklore carefully constructed around him and his relation to other threatening childhood figures (particularly Heinrich Hoffmann's *Struwwelpeter*) truly is the boogeyman. Opening with a scene that shows Krueger fashioning his knife-fingered glove by infernal firelight in his filthy and half-flooded boiler room before terrorising a night-dress-clad Tina, Craven encapsulates both the Gothic and Grimm's fairy tale elements that, however sub-consciously, inflected the slasher movie. The other obvious reference is to Frankenstein's monster. In his 'filthy workshop of creation' Krueger becomes both his own and the Elm Street parents' Frankenstein's monster. Ironically, it would prove to be the same with Craven and Krueger - the monster eventually overshadowing his creator and far exceeding his intentions.

As in most slashers, the authority figures here are weak but they are rendered doubly so by their complicity in Krueger's death - a pact of silence for an act that the law would not sanction. The parents' denials, first that anything is wrong and then of Krueger's survival, only increase his powers over their children. *A Nightmare On Elm Street* approaches the threat of the boogeyman from the opposite end. Whereas parents usually threaten their children with him to encourage good behaviour, their refusal of him here encourages their children to 'misbehave' - i.e. staying up late, leaving the house without permission and so on - until Nancy's parents take the step of putting bars on the windows to keep Nancy in and thus force her to confront 'the boogeyman.'

Langenkamp, who previously appeared in Francis Ford Coppola's adaptations of S E Hinton's *The Outsiders* (1983) and *Rumble Fish* (1983) makes a splendid final girl - driven, chaste, intelligent and strong-willed. She continually pushes her parents despite their denials and finally gets answers. When Glen notices her reading matter, *"Booby Traps And Anti-Personnel Devices?"* she replies, "I'm into survival." More impressive is her final exorcism of Krueger. By turning her back on him and denying both his existence and her part in the collective uncon-scious that he inhabits, he is expelled. (But only until the tacked-on end-ing to allow for sequels). Now that's strength!

Fred Krueger, meanwhile, is never more threatening than in this first movie (until its postmodern reworking *Wes Craven's New Nightmare* (see later)). Played by Englund, previously best known for his role as the friendly, bubble-permed alien in *V*, his lines here are restricted to unpleas-antness such as, "I'm gonna kill you slow," rather than the cracker-barrel clowning that later sequels would encourage. Here his performance, com-bined with Craven's exploitation of dream-logic - the staircase that turns to immobilising goo, beds and baths sucking in victims, the tongue com-ing out of the phone receiver to lick Nancy's face - help to make *A Night-mare On Elm Street* extremely powerful, both as a slasher movie and as an updated fairy tale.

Verdict: 4/5

Unfortunately, a tacked-on twist ending, allowed New Line to exploit their new-found success and there seemed to be a limitless supply of teenagers on Elm Street.

A Nightmare On Elm Street 2 - Freddy's Revenge (1986) is a hasty sequel with tortured teen Jesse moving into Nancy's old house and having nightmares that help Freddy Krueger possess him and find further victims. A distasteful homophobic subtext lurks beneath the slaughter of the SM-loving coach and Jesse's best friend, especially as the love of a good woman saves Jesse from Freddy's attentions. Director Jack Sholder previously edited *The Burning* and went on to direct cult SF-thriller *The Hidden* (1988). *Verdict:* 1/5

A Nightmare On Elm Street 3 - Dream Warriors (1987) A clinic for suicidal teens becomes the latest target of Freddy's attentions. Nancy returns to help the teens use their dream-powers against him and it is revealed that Freddy's mother was a nun who conceived him after being raped by a hundred maniacs whilst trapped overnight in an asylum. Lt Thompson unearths Krueger's remains so that he can be laid to rest but both he and Nancy are killed. Despite the loss of several friends, Final Girl Kristen (Patricia Arquette) takes Freddy down. Director Chuck Russell, ironically, had written the script for the *Nightmare*-similar *Dreamscape*; he achieved mainstream success with *The Mask* (1994) starring Jim Carrey. *Verdict:* 3/5

Originally scripted by Craven (with Bruce Wagner), *Dream Warriors* saw the last of his involvement until *Wes Craven's New Nightmare* (1988), because of drastic changes made to his original idea. *A Nightmare On Elm Street 4* saw Robert Englund achieve pre-title-credit status and, by appearing as an Aurora model-kit (a position only awarded to Universal Studio's monsters), introducing his *Tales From The Crypt*-style TV series *Freddy's Nightmares* and rapping with the Fat Boys, Englund's Freddy Krueger became the iconic monster of the 80s. This also meant that Fred Krueger now became a punning master of ceremonies for increasingly elaborate set piece surrealist death sequences (teenagers turned into cockroaches, motorcycles, etc.) that had little impact beyond looking technically impressive. Any atmosphere was drowned out by power-rock tracks that would pad out the accompanying soundtrack album.

A Nightmare On Elm Street 4 - The Dream Master (1988). Directed by soon-to-be action movie maestro Renny Harlin and co-scripted by *Payback* (1998) director Brian Helgeland, Freddy Krueger is resurrected thanks to a fire-pissing dog (I kid you not) and, after killing off the teens who survived *Dream Warriors* among others, meets his match in Alice (Lisa Wilcox) who has become the Dream Master by absorbing her dead friends' special attributes. *Verdict:* 1/5

A Nightmare On Elm Street 5 - The Dream Child (1989, director Stephen Hopkins). The teen-pregnancy episode as Alice realises Krueger is returning through the dreams of her unborn child. Ripping off everything from *Psycho* (guess which scene), through to *It's Alive!* (1976), via M C Escher and the video for Aha's 'Take on Me,' Krueger is destroyed this time by the laying to rest of his mother's earthly remains. *Verdict:* 2/5

Freddy's Dead - The Final Nightmare (1991). Directed by Rachel Talalay, who had worked in a production capacity on most of the previous episodes and went on to direct the appalling *Tank Girl* (1995), this is the one with the 3-D ending (retained on the video release), cameos by Johnny Depp and Roseanne Barr and very little else to recommend it. Freddy, seeking a permanent return to the real world, is finally destroyed by his daughter, whose existence had been kept a secret until the script for this shambles was being cobbled together. *Verdict:* 3/5 - but only because of the 3-D

As Wes Craven's original vision became increasingly debased and the *Friday The 13th* franchise struggled to keep abreast of the competition, there was one film that managed to sum up the whole slasher industry. Whereas the early 80s boom had produced lame parodies such as *Wacko!* (1981), *Student Bodies* (1981) and *National Lampoon's Class Reunion* (1982, scripted by John Hughes), which tried to poke fun at the genre without realising that laughter was part of the package in the first place, *Return To Horror High* made the industry that produced such films the butt of its humour.

Return To Horror High (1987)

Cast: Lori Lethin (Callie/Sarah/Susan), Brendan Hughes (Steven Blake), Alex Rocco (Harry Sleerik), Scott Jacoby (Josh Forbes), Andy Romano (Principal Kastleman), Richard Brestoff (Arthur Lymam), Al Fann (Amos), Pepper Martin (Chief Deyner), Maureen McCormack (Officer Tyler), Vince Edwards (Richard Birnbaum), Philip McKean (Richard Farley), Panchito Gomez (Choo Choo), George Clooney (Oliver)

Crew: Director Bill Froelich, Producer Mark Lisson, Writers Bill Froelich & Mark Lisson & Dana Escalante & Greg H Sims, Cinematography Roy Wagner, Music

Story: Called to a crime scene at Crippen High School, the police find the area littered with body parts. The only survivor of the slaughter, scriptwriter Arthur Lymam, tells them how he was part of a crew from Cosmic Pictures who have been filming a reconstruction of the massacre that took place at the school five years before... Slipping between flashbacks to the film set and to the original events, the tale begins to unfold. Due to budget cuts, cast and crew are living at the school. Some of the cast are playing themselves, including Steven Blake, a policeman who was first on the scene, janitor Amos (the sound of whose squeaking bucket-on-wheels pervades the school) and Principal Kastleman who, after several members of the cast go missing, is finally unmasked by Blake and Callie as the killer. Kastleman was murdering anyone who had ever tried to touch his daughter. Blake manages to kill him with a javelin but, according to Arthur: "They never got out." The police go in to investigate and, sounding the all-clear, the actors and crew climb out from under their sheets. Satisfied that they have got the final scene and unmasked the killer, they all drive off, leaving the police to wonder what is going on. However, Arthur turns out to be Kastleman's son and begins work on a sequel, entitled *Return To Horror High*, vowing: "No rewrites next time."

Background: In a similar vein to films such as *Frankenstein 1970* (1958), and *House Of Seven Corpses* (1974) in that it features the making of a film beset by murders (a plot that would later be taken up by *Scream 3*), *Return To Horror High* uses this scenario to examine both the nature of the audience's relationships to violence on screen and the restrictions imposed on creativity by the exploitation film industry. No relation to *Horror High* (1974), which was a tale of psychic revenge set at a high school, it is also the title of the film that Cosmic Pictures are making. Whilst sometimes over-reaching itself a little, *Return To Horror High* remains the high point of the parodies that emerged from the slasher boom because, rather than reducing everything to farce, it plays the actual horror straight, an approach it shares with the equally impressive *Texas Chainsaw* parody *Motel Hell* (1980, director Kevin Connor). *Return To Horror High*'s murders and the climactic discovery of Kastleman's skeletal classroom could have come from any competently-handled slasher flick. Arthur's explanations to the police are both convincing and amusing. No one missed the disappearing cast and crew because it is a low-budget film: "You get used to working with less." Likewise, no one notices the blood because it's a horror film: "Everything was covered in blood by the end of the first week."

The audience is constantly wrong-footed by scenes that appear to be flashbacks to the original murders but turn out to be reconstructions; a boom mike drops into view, policeman Blake complains that the scene is not accurate. Most notably this occurs when, during an intense rape scene between the first two 'victims,' the producer's hand appears to make sure the actress' breasts are in shot. The scene is then further disrupted by Callie's outraged response about exploitation films only ever exploiting women. "You'll be icing my nipples to make sure they stand up next!" she accuses. The man with the ice immediately turns and leaves the set. Sincere director Forbes continually confronts exploitative producer Harry Sleerik over his insistence at more tits and gore in a knowing echo of working for Roger Corman's New World company (who co-produced the picture) and, needless to say, everyone takes it out on Arthur, the harassed writer. "You'd better write something redeeming," Sleerik tells him, asking for yet another rewrite following Callie's outburst, "Two girls just talking about life, love, babies...You know. And set it in the locker-room shower so they're naked." Corman should have sued.

Memorable Lines: 1) Director (railing against his producer's demands): "There will be *no* exploding tit shot!" 2) Actor: "What's my motivation?" Director: "You're *dead*. Dead people don't have any motivation!"

Verdict: 5/5

7. Flowing Into The Mainstream

"We are going to keep this family together!"

Jerry Blake, *The Stepfather.*

Following the commercial and critical success of the *A Nightmare On Elm Street* series, the influence of the slasher genre began to cross over to more mainstream thrillers. Serial killer movies such as Robert Harmon's *The Hitcher* (1986) and Michael Mann's *Manhunter* (1986) emerge. At the same time the standard slasher formula continued to stagger on, not just in the form of sequels but in pallid copies such as *Sorority House Massacre* (1986), *April Fool's Day* (1986), *Slaughter High* (1987, aka *April Fool's Day*), *Intruder* (1988) and *Popcorn* (1991). The previous critical opprobrium that had kept many major studios from jumping on the slasher bandwagon changed with the success of *Fatal Attraction*. This film managed to have its cake and eat it, in that it was not generally perceived as a horror movie (and, in particular, not a slasher movie), yet stole wholeheartedly from the genre's conventions. Many such films followed, predominantly described as 'thrillers,' using large stars, big budgets and usually the same conventions. What makes such films problematic is that, by adding more 'social' concerns to the stories in order to distance themselves from the psychotic monsters of the slashers, these films tended to strike a far more reactionary chord than their predecessors.

Fatal Attraction (1987)

Cast: Michael Douglas (Dan Gallagher), Glenn Close (Alex Forrest), Anne Archer (Beth Gallagher), Fred Gwynne (Arthur), Mike Nussbaum (Bob Drimmer), Stuart Pankin (Jimmy), Ellen Foley (Hildy), Ellen Hamilton Lantzen (Ellen Gallagher), Lois Smith (Martha), Meg Munday (Joan Rogerson), Tom Brennan (Howard Rogerson), JJ Johnson (O'Rourke), Michael Arkin (Lieutenant), Sam J Coppola (Fusselli)

Crew: Director Adrian Lyne, Producers Stanley R Jaffe & Sherry Lansing, Writer James Dearden, Cinematography Howard Atherton, Music Maurice Jarre, Editors Michael Kahn & Peter E Berger, Production Designer Mel Bourne, 120 minutes

Story: After a brief sexual liaison with Alex Forrest, an editor working for a company represented by his law firm, Dan Gallagher goes back to his perfect family: Beth, his wife, and their daughter Ellen. When his wife is away, Dan is drawn back for a second night. At Alex's apartment that evening, Dan tells her it is the end - Alex slashes her wrists. Dan nurses her, ensures she is okay and leaves. However, Alex pursues him, and tells him she is pregnant and she is going to keep the baby despite Dan's attempts to convince her to have an abortion. She continues to harass Dan. Dan gets his home phone number changed and Alex shows up to see his wife, Beth, feigning interest in buying their apartment. The family move to a new house in the country. After further threats from Alex, the family come home to find Ellen's rabbit has been boiled alive in a saucepan. Dan confesses to Beth and when Alex phones Beth answers and threatens her with violence. Alex then kidnaps Ellen, which indirectly results in Beth having a car accident. When Ellen is returned safely, Dan visits Alex and they fight. Later, Alex turns up at his house and tries to kill Beth. Dan drowns her in the bathtub but she comes back for one last 'Boo!' whereupon Beth shoots her. The film ends with a family portrait of Dan, Beth and Ellen.

Background: Fatal Attraction was the big horror movie of the 80s, but few people realised it was a horror movie, thinking of it as a tawdry rewrite of Clint Eastwood's *Play Misty For Me* (1971). However, here the 'hero' is excused his dalliance rather than criticised for it because early on in the movie Alex is shown to be madder than a box of hot frogs. While Lyne executes the sex-everywhere-but-in-bed scenes and the *Fri-*

day The 13th conclusion with his usual slickness, the rest of the film mainly consists of Alex phoning Dan and him telling her to stop it. The authorities here are as hopeless as ever, hands tied by ridiculous laws that stop them from arresting people unless an actual crime is committed. The film's original conclusion, which had Alex committing suicide and pinning the blame on Dan, was drastically altered after preview audiences gave it the thumbs down. The reshot version allowed Dan to get off scot-free, united with Beth in defending their home against the monster. The phrase 'bunny-boiler' has now entered the vernacular to describe a woman whose social behaviour does not conform to the expected 'norm'.

Verdict: 1/5

The enormous box-office success of *Fatal Attraction* spawned many variations on the same theme from other major studios: *Sleeping With The Enemy* (1991) starred Julia Roberts under threat from her vicious control-freak husband (Patrick Bergin); *The Hand That Rocks The Cradle* (1991) has vengeance-seeking Rebecca De Mornay visiting the middle-class family that caused her husband's suicide thus ruining her own middle-class life; *Pacific Heights* (1990) and *Unlawful Entry* (1992) saw couples Matthew Modine and Melanie Griffiths, and Kurt Russell and Madeleine Stowe defending their lives and properties against psycho-tenant Michael Keaton and psycho-cop Ray Liotta, respectively; the slightly more subtle, but no less reactionary *Single White Female* (1992) found Bridget Fonda struggling to stop her identity being stolen by room-mate-from-hell Jennifer Jason Leigh. The pseudo-slashers in what became known as the 'cuckoo-in-the-nest' cycle espoused family values surprisingly similar to Terry O'Quinn's in *The Stepfather*. This lower-budget but far more subversive movie was released in the UK shortly before *Fatal Attraction* and was smothered by that film's success.

The Stepfather (1986)

Cast: Terry O'Quinn (Jerry Blake), Shelley Hack (Susan), Jill Schoelen (Stephanie), Charles Lanyer (Dr Bondurant), Stephen Shellen (Jim Ogilvie), Stephen E Miller (Al Brennan)

Crew: Director Joseph Rubin, Producer Jay Benson, Writers Donald E Westlake & Carolyn Lefcourt & Brian Garfield, Cinematography John W Lindley, Music Patrick Moraz, Editor George Bowers, Production Designer James William Newport, Special Effects Bill Orr, 98 minutes

Story: Jerry Blake is a psychopath whose obsession with belonging to the perfect family means he focuses on single mothers and moves in. If the family does not hold together, he changes his identity, establishes a new job and life for himself, then butchers the old family and slips away to his new one. Now living with widowed Susan and her daughter Stephanie, Jerry is unaware that he is being tracked by his vengeful old brother-in-law, Jim Ogilvie. Meanwhile, his relationship with stepdaughter Stephanie becomes increasingly strained as he tries to impose his ideals upon her. She becomes increasingly suspicious of his rages, especially when she hears of the serial killer who murders families. Discovering Stephanie's suspicions about him, Jerry at first tries to placate her and keep the family together but one row too many makes him realise that it is time to start afresh. Secretly quitting his job, he begins to establish his next identity and is soon ready to get rid of the old. However, he does not reckon on Stephanie's resourcefulness.

Background: Ex-TV director Ruben, who had previously directed *Dreamscape*, a political thriller closely resembling *A Nightmare On Elm Street* (a fact that did not escape Wes Craven's attentions), here directs a surprisingly taut black comedy. *The Stepfather* is a subversive affair, with brutal shocks and a truly impressive central performance from Terry O'Quinn as the Norman Rockwell wannabe whose tantrums in his workroom have to be seen to be believed. Made at a time when politicians both in the US and the UK were preaching a return to the family values of the 50s, the notion of the nuclear family as the American ideal comes under particular close scrutiny here. Single mom Hack and daughter Schoelen seem perfectly happy until Jerry shows up and starts to impose his will. Unlike *Fatal Attraction* and many of the cuckoo-in-the-nest movies of similar ilk where the perfect family unit expels the monster and regroups despite the battering, *The Stepfather* suggests that this perfect family unit may often be the seat of the monster, a threat to all concerned. Therefore the family 'norm' needs to be questioned. Much play is made of Jerry's understanding of the 'family' through references to idealised representations on TV programmes such as *Leave It To Beaver*, and Jerry's reactions to situations where people (particularly stepdaughter Schoelen) refuse to fit into the pigeon-holes that he has constructed for them. The film's shock opening means we know full well how dangerous Jerry can be and the suspense in waiting for him to finally boil over often becomes unbearable. The scenes where he grills the psychiatrist, who pretends to be an interested real-estate client, and later, when he realises he has lost track of which identity he is using, are especially unnerving.

Verdict: 4/5

The Stepfather spawned two sequels. *The Stepfather II* (1990) also starred O'Quinn. This time posing as a family counsellor and courting

Meg Foster, the film retained the original's off-kilter sense of humour. The gorier and less impressive *Stepfather III* (1992) was shot for cable TV and replaced O'Quinn, via plastic surgery, with Robert Wightman, who ends up being fed into a wood-shredder.

Despite two haphazard and extremely belated attempts to revive Michael Myers: *Halloween 4 - The Return Of Michael Myers* (1988) and *Halloween 5* (1989), both of which centre on Michael's attempts to find and kill his newly-discovered niece, Jamie (played by Danielle Harris) and portray him as a supernatural version of Rambo, the teen slasher movie had become outmoded. Proof of this came in 1991 when one film emerged which would appropriate the slasher genre's conventions to a level of success previously unimagined.

The Silence Of The Lambs (1991)

Cast: Jodie Foster (Clarice Starling), Anthony Hopkins (Hannibal Lecter), Scott Glenn (Jack Crawford), Ted Levine (Jame Gumb/Buffalo Bill), Anthony Heald (Dr Frederick Chilton), Charles Napier (Lt Boyle), Kasi Lemmons (Ardelia Mapp), Brooke Smith (Catherine Martin), Tracey Walter (Lamar), Diane Baker (Senator Ruth Martin), Roger Corman (FBI Director Hayden Burke)

Crew: Director Jonathan Demme, Producers Edward Saxon & Kenneth Utt & Ron Bozman, Writer Ted Tally, Novel Thomas Harris, Cinematography Tak Fujimoto, Music Howard Shore, Editor Craig McKay, Production Designer Kristi Zea, Special Make-Up Effects Carl Fullerton & Neal Martz, 119 minutes

Story: FBI trainee Clarice Starling is sent by her superior Jack Crawford to interview serial killer Hannibal 'The Cannibal' Lecter, an insane but civilised genius. From his cell, Lecter offers to exchange insights relating to a murder spree for Clarice's personal secrets. The murderer in question, Buffalo Bill, kidnaps and skins young women. His latest victim, currently starving in his basement, is the daughter of a prominent senator who exerts pressure on Crawford to crack the case, even to the extent of offering Lecter a deal. Interference from Lecter's keeper, the egotistical Dr Chilton, provides Lecter with the opportunity to escape and Clarice is left to follow other leads which take her straight to Bill's lair.

Background: The first horror film to win an Oscar for best picture (it also won Oscars for Demme, Foster and Hopkins) *The Silence Of The Lambs*, despite its plaudits, remains a big-budget slasher movie. Hannibal Lecter is, for all his intelligence, another slasher-movie monster. Like Freddie Krueger, he is prone to bad puns ("I'm having an old friend for dinner," he phones to tell Clarice, as he stalks Dr Chilton) and licking his chops in a villainous manner. Clarice Starling is the final girl *par excellence*, married to her FBI job, intelligent, capable of protecting herself and always one step ahead of anyone else in the law-enforcement game. The film's authority figures, Scott Glenn's FBI father figure, Anthony

Heald's Dr Chilton and Charles Napier's Lt Boyle, provide little support for Clarice. It is Clarice who discovers the moth larva in the corpse's throat, solves Lecter's little riddles and bests Buffalo Bill, despite his 'supernatural' power of night-vision goggles. Bill, a combination of real-life serial killers Ted Bundy (he uses Bundy's technique of pretending to have a broken arm to dispel any threat he might pose to his victims) and that slasher favourite, Ed Gein (again, Bill is represented as a mother-obsessive, who is killing and skinning women to make a 'woman-suit'), caused problems for the gay community who saw his character as homophobic, in much the same way that Sharon Stone's bisexual character in *Basic Instinct* (1992) came under attack. However, Bill is pointedly described as not being gay in the scene where Starling discusses the nature of the beast with Glenn. In the best tradition of the psychiatrist's speech at the end of *Psycho*, Bill's behaviour is understood as a desire for change, hence the symbol of the moth larva. Brian Cox gave a more chillingly calm portrayal of Lecter in Michael Mann's *Manhunter* (1986), an adaptation of Thomas Harris' earlier book *Red Dragon*, which introduced Lecter's character.

Verdict: 3/5

Thus accepted by the movie industry, the serial-killer film, part horror/part police procedural, would become a dominant sub-genre of the 90s. Films such as *Se7en* (1994) (David Fincher's nihilistic reworking of *The Abominable Dr Phibes* (1970)), Jon Amiel's hysterical *Copycat* (1995) and Gregory Hoblit's demonic slasher *Fallen* (1997) pit big star names such as Brad Pitt, Morgan Freeman, Holly Hunter, Sigourney Weaver and Denzel Washington against fiendish killers in plots that increasingly tried to distance themselves from their slasher heritage.

8. The Return Of The Slasher

"And this is the scene where the killer comes back for one last scare"
Sidney Prescott - *Scream*

The mainstream slasher continued to plough the same comfortable ruts. Evidence of this can easily be found in the virtually interchangeable smart cop/smarter serial killer retreads that continue to be released. For example, Morgan Freeman and Ashley Judd in the adaptation of James Patterson's *Kiss The Girls* (1997), Rutger Hauer in the prurient *Bone Daddy* (1998), and Denzel Washington as the quadriplegic detective in *The Bone Collector* (1999). The slasher movie slipped away briefly, the monsters of the 80s seemingly found their final resting places: Jason in a New York sewer, Freddy Krueger blown apart by his daughter, Leatherface and Michael Myers missing in action. There were, however, changes afoot. The first was Sean S Cunningham's beefed-up revamp of the *Friday The 13th* franchise.

Jason Goes To Hell - The Final Friday (1993)

Cast: John D LeMay (Steven Freeman), Kari Keegan (Jessica Kimble), Allison Smith (Vicki), Steven Culp (Robert Campbell), Billy Green Bush (Sheriff Landis), Rusty Schwimmer (Joey B), Leslie Jordan (Shelby), Andrew Bloch (Josh), Kipp Marcus (Randy), Richard Gant (Coroner), Adam Cranner (Ward), Julie Michaels (Elizabeth Marcus FBI), Kane Hodder (Jason Voorhees), Erin Gray (Diana Kimble), Steven Williams (Creighton Duke)

Crew: Director Adam Marcus, Producer Sean S Cunningham, Writers Jay Huguely & Adam Marcus (story) & Dean Lorey & Jay Huguely (screenplay), Cinematography William Dill, Editor David Handman, Music Harry Manfredini, Production Designer W Brooke Wheeler, Special Make-Up Effects Robert Kurtzmann & Greg Nicotero & Howard Berger (KNB EFX Group), Special Visual Effects Al Magliochetti, 84 minutes

Story: Decoyed into a trap, Jason is blown up by the army. Unfortunately, the force inside him possesses the coroner and continues on its killing spree. Tracked by bounty hunter Creighton Duke, who knows that Jason can only be properly reborn through or destroyed by his blood relatives, he warns Jason's sister Diana Kimble to protect her daughter Jessica and her baby. As the force switches from victim to victim, Diana is killed and Jason reborn, setting the scene for a final showdown between him and his niece.

Background: Now owned by New Line Cinema who, as well as holding the franchise to the *A Nightmare On Elm Street* series had dallied briefly with Leatherface in *The Texas Chainsaw Massacre 3*, *Jason Goes To Hell* was the first in the series since the original *Friday The 13th* that involved Sean S Cunningham. Given that he had distanced himself from the project since Paramount started bankrolling the franchise, this involvement suggests a certain amount of score-settling and, indeed, there are certainly references in the film that confirm this view. Starting in true slasher fashion with an attractive woman arriving at Crystal Lake only to undress and start taking a shower, the scene is revealed to be a set-up to lure Jason out to be blown to smithereens.

Knowing references to the usual *Friday The 13th* formula are highlighted by a character's comment to three teenager campers, heading out to Crystal Lake now that Jason has been pronounced dead: "So, you guys planning on smoking a little dope, having a little premarital sex and getting slaughtered?" Needless to say, they do, but as if to rub our noses in it, the couple within the trio also have *unprotected* premarital sex. The script also has several digs at America's fascination with murder through the true-crime TV genre: Campbell's amoral American Casebook presenter cheerfully moves Diana Kimble's body to the Voorhees house so the police can 'discover' it live on TV; and a diner advertises a 'Jason is Dead 2 for 1 burger sale' (the burgers are cut into the shapes of hockey masks).

What raises the plot above the ordinary *Friday The 13th* line is a device lifted wholesale from Jack Sholder's more interesting SF/horror *The Hidden* (1983) - jumping from body to body. (For other uses of this device see Stephen Gallagher's earlier novel *Valley Of Lights* and the demonic serial-killer flick *Fallen* (1998)). Jason, it seems, derives his supernatural powers from a demon that inhabits his body, and the only chance we have of being saved from him rests in the figure of his previously unheard-of niece. As with Freddy Krueger and Michael Myers before him, Jason's relatives seem to crawl out of the woodwork whenever the tired formula needs a kick-start, and the family must struggle to expel the black sheep.

However, although derivative, *Jason Goes To Hell* is well paced and very violent (although the UK version is the 'soft' US version where the most brutal deaths were filmed from a less overt angle). This film showed that like *Return To Horror High* (1987), someone had at least tried to come up with a different spin on the traditional slasher movie. One major disappointment remains. Jason does indeed go to Hell, but the ending is marred by the inclusion of a plot twist which had previously only been the subject of discussion in gore magazines such as *Fangoria* since the mid-80s - speculations about who would win should one slasher be pitted against another in much the same fashion as *Godzilla Vs. King Kong*, or *Frankenstein Meets The Wolfman*. In the final shot we see Jason's hockey mask laying on the ground. As it is about to sink out of view, a clawed hand in a stripy jersey reaches out and grabs it.

Memorable Line: "That thing's in the basement with Jessica's mother!"

Verdict: 4/5

Despite the possibility of being pitted against Jason, Fred Krueger had other issues to resolve, especially that of his own comeback in...

Wes Craven's New Nightmare (1994)

Cast: Robert Englund (Himself/ Freddy Krueger), Heather Langenkamp, John Saxon, Wes Craven, Marianne Maddelena, Sam Rubin, Sara Risher, Robert Shaye, Nick Corri, Tuesday Knight (themselves), Miko Hughes (Dylan), David Newsom (Chase Porter), Tracy Middendorff (Julie), Fran Bennett (Dr Heffner), Matt Winston (Chuck), Rob LaBelle (Terry)

Crew: Director/Writer Wes Craven, Producer Marianne Maddalena, Cinematography Mark Irwin, Music J Peter Robinson, Editor Patrick Lussier, Production Designer Cynthia Charette, Special Make-Up Effects Kurtzmann, Nicotero, Berger EFX Group & David Miller, 112 minutes

Story: Ten years after starring in *A Nightmare On Elm Street*, Heather Langenkamp is now married to special effects man Chase and has a small son, Dylan. Suffering from bad dreams and receiving phone calls from a Freddy Krueger sound-alike, she is summoned to New Line's offices where Robert Shaye offers her the lead in a new film being written by Wes Craven. The film, Craven explains, will bring back Freddy, revealing him as the manifestation of an ancient evil which has appeared throughout history. This evil can only be bound when held inside a successful story and since the end of the *Elm Street* series, this evil has been released into the real world. After Heather dreams of Chase's death, which then comes true, she becomes convinced that Freddy is trying to enter the real world through Dylan, who is acting oddly. When taken into hospital for tests, the doctor's dislike of horror films makes her suspect Heather's parenting abilities and, finding Dylan is suffering from sleep deprivation, sedates him. Falling under Freddy's power, Dylan escapes from the hospital. Heather turns to her friend John Saxon for help but he acts as if he is her father, the role he played in *A Nightmare On Elm Street*. Back on Elm Street once more, Heather finally defeats Freddy with Dylan's help and Craven's completed screenplay removes Freddy from reality.

Background: Both praised and slated at the time of its release, *Wes Craven's New Nightmare* can be seen as a small triumph for the film-maker who had created the franchise only to see it taken away from him and be watered down until it died as slow a death as Krueger himself. The film came about after New Line executive Robert Shaye had finally buried the hatchet concerning the company's poor treatment (both financially and artistically) of Craven. Finally recompensed, Craven reacted positively to scripting a new sequel for the company. Even so, that New Line allowed *Wes Craven's New Nightmare* to be made is a triumph in itself especially since the film throws in barbed comments about their previous marketing of the monster. For example, in the scene where Craven explains that Krueger is an expression of evil in the shared unconscious and makes a reasonable attempt to construct a serious discussion about the very nature of why people enjoy horror movies, behind him we can see an Andy Warhol-style screen print of Krueger amongst other Freddy paraphernalia. In another scene, in a TV show appearance Langenkamp is unexpectedly menaced by Robert Englund dressed as Freddy while the audience all cheer and wave their Freddy gloves.

In *New Nightmare* Krueger is again the scowling, snarling beast of the first *Elm Street* movie rather than the pun-spouting star-turn that he became in the later sequels. Craven, Robert Shaye, Englund, Langenkamp and Saxon all have fun playing themselves while the scenes where the actors find themselves trapped back in their Elm Street roles manage to be genuinely unsettling. Despite a lukewarm reception at the box office, Craven would return to the same territory two years later.

Verdict: 4/5

Serial-killer movies had reached their height with films such as David Fincher's *Se7en* (1996), and John Waters' parody *Serial Mom* (1994). The themes of the cuckoo-in-the-nest film cycle had become established as part of a sub-genre, the 'based on a true story' TV movie format. The 'pure' slasher movie looked set to become a footnote in horror genre history and film studies courses. After all, how far could an 80s horror trend be stretched? A little further, it turned out, with the arrival of a script by an ex-actor whose only previous script, *Killing Mrs Tingle*, had been stuck in 'development hell' for over a year. The title of the script was *Scary Movie*, the writer Kevin Williamson, and the resulting movie would grant a small but rewarding reprieve for the unmourned slasher.

Scream (1997)

Cast: Neve Campbell (Sidney Prescott), David Arquette (Deputy Dwight 'Dewey' Riley), Courtney Cox (Gale Weathers), Matthew Lillard (Stuart), Rose McGowan (Tatum Riley), Skeet Ulrich (Billy Loomis), Drew Barrymore (Casey Becker), Jamie Kennedy (Randy), Liev Schreiber (Cotton Weary), Henry Winkler (Principal Himbry, uncredited), Linda Blair (Reporter, uncredited)

Crew: Director Wes Craven, Producers Cary Woods & Cathy Konrad, Writer Kevin Williamson, Cinematography Mark Irwin & Peter Deming, Music Marco Beltrami, Editor Patrick Lussier, Production Designer Bruce Alan Miller, Special Make-Up Effects Kurtzman, Nicotero and Berger EFX Group, 111 minutes

Story: A spectre is haunting the sleepy town of Woodsboro. It is a murderous psychopath who torments his victims with phone calls about scary movies before killing them. His main target for torment, however, seems to be teenager Sidney Prescott, whose mother Maureen had been murdered the previous year. The man presumed responsible, Maureen's lover Cotton Weary, was identified by Sidney and jailed. Reporter Gale Weathers believes him to be innocent and, despite much animosity between her, Sidney and Deputy 'Dewey' Riley and carnage at a house party, the killers are finally unmasked.

Background: For anyone who grew up with the films that *Scream* comments on, deconstructs and replays, it is well-nigh perfect. For those who have never seen a slasher movie in their lives, it should scare the bejesus out of you. While Craven and Williamson manage to fill scenes with riffs and intertextual comments on the slasher genre, they never forget that the reason the audience is there is to see a scary movie (the original title is still vastly superior but perhaps too knowing to have drawn the box office *Scream* did). The opening cat-and-mouse sequence between the superbly ghost-masked killer and Barrymore's Casey is particularly harrowing.

Nowhere is *Scream*'s delight in its own referenciality more evident than in the scene where Randy, the movie nerd, after commentating on *Halloween* for the benefit of the now-departed party-goers, tells the on-screen Jamie Lee Curtis to 'Look behind you!,' at the same time that the murderer is lurking behind him. In the next scene we see that Randy is being filmed in the OB van where, on a time delay, Kenny is watching Randy and echoes Randy's words right back at him, between which points the audience have most likely done likewise. However, the dissection of the sub-genre never gets in the way of the shocks or the elements that anyone who has seen *Halloween* and *Friday The 13th* expects and loves. So we get imaginative deaths (Rose McGowan trapped in a cat flap in an opening garage door), we get ineffectual authority figures (Sidney's dad and Dewey, the sweetest hopeless cop ever), we get a cool-looking psycho and we get Sidney, a final girl's final girl. We are also treated to a neatly self-deprecating cameo by Craven who, wearing a battered hat and a green-and-red-striped jersey plays Fred, the janitor.

Scream is populated by a cast who, rather than the usual awkward unknowns never seen again, had already proved their mettle. A cast that would go on to bigger things, something that would be notable in this revival of the genre. Neve Campbell had come from the teen TV-soap series *Party Of Five*, Courtney Cox from *Friends*, McGowan, Lillard and Schreiber had all worked in small but memorable indie films - *The Doom Generation*, *Serial Mom* and *The Daytrippers*, respectively, and then there's poor old Drew Barrymore.

Memorable Lines: Billy Loomis: "Films don't make psychos, they just make psychos more creative."

Verdict: 5/5

I Know What You Did Last Summer (1997)

Cast: Jennifer Love Hewitt (Julie James), Sarah Michelle Gellar (Helen Shivers), Ryan Phillippe (Barry Cox), Freddie Prinze Jr (Ray Bronson), Johnny Galecki (Max), Bridgette Wilson (Elsa Shivers), Anne Heche (Melissa Egan), Muse Watson (Benjamin Willis/Fisherman)

Crew: Director Jim Gillespie, Producers Neal H Moritz & Erik Feig & Stokely Chaffin, Writer Kevin Williamson, Novel Lois Duncan, Cinematography Denis Crossan, Music John Debney, Editor Steve Mirkovich, Production Designer Gary Wissner, Special Make-Up Effects Matthew W Mungle & Jamie Kelman, 101 minutes

Story: After killing a fisherman in a hit-and-run accident, four teenage high school graduates vow to keep it secret. They dispose of the body in the sea and attempt to get on with their lives. The next summer, however, the four receive threatening letters and, one by one, they begin to fall victim to a vicious hook-wielding killer in fisherman's garb. They try to uncover the identity of the hit-and-run victim before it's too late.

Background: Kevin Williamson's second slasher script was for Columbia, who were sued by Miramax for using the advertising tagline 'From the creator of *Scream.*' *I Know What You Did Last Summer* is far more traditional fare. Adapted from a popular teenage novel, the movie offers scares and sympathetic teens but lacks the postmodern knowingness of *Scream.* (The exception was the scene where Hewitt and Gellar visit a suspect's house in the sticks. They use false names, Angela and Jodie, after jokily comparing their situation to *Murder, She Wrote* and *Silence Of The Lambs.*) Williamson's script takes time to establish the impact of one night of tragedy on the characters' lives, and the portrayal of Gellar's promising student reduced to working in the family store with her catty sister is the most poignant. Elsewhere the standard disappearing body business and red herrings play as well as they ever did, but the evil fisherman in his waterproofs is pure *Scooby-Doo* and the twist ending seems as arbitrarily sequel-foreboding as anything from the early 80s.

Verdict: 2/5

It should come as no surprise that *I Still Know What You Did Last Summer* (1998) appeared. Also starring Hewitt and Prinze Jr., it was directed by Danny Cannon, presumably trying to make box-office amends after the disastrous *Judge Dredd* (1995). Set on a storm-tossed Caribbean island, the evil fisherman continues to torment Julie and Ray but fails to off co-star Brandy. He is also revealed to have a psychotic son. Appalling. *Verdict:* 0/5

Michael Myers was resurrected once more in 1995, for the half-witted *Halloween - The Curse Of Michael Myers*, (which was, presumably, "bloody hell, not again"). Here, along with some malarkey about a druid-cult, he finally kills now-teenaged Jamie and pursues her baby, being protected by a grown-up Tommy, Laurie's baby-sitting charge in the original *Halloween*. Aided by Loomis (an ill-looking Donald Pleasence who was to die shortly after filming was completed), Tommy kills Michael and takes Jamie's baby to safety. Michael, however, comes back and kills Loomis. *Verdict:* 0/5

Then came *Halloween H20 - Twenty Years Later* (1998), which involved Kevin Williamson as executive producer and script-doctor. This is a glossy-looking follow-up directed by Steve Miner, with the return of Jamie Lee Curtis and featuring a brief but knowing cameo by Jamie's mom, Janet Leigh. Pleasingly, *Halloween H20* is written as if the previous three sequels had never happened (would that it were true). Laurie, now in her 30s, has changed her name to Keri Tate and is the principal of the same school her teenaged son, John, attends. Battling both with her memories and with her alcohol consumption, Laurie is unaware that Michael has killed Marion (the late Dr Loomis' assistant) and uncovered her new identity. Needless to say, it all degenerates into teen-killing but director Miner remembers to include plenty of corner-of-the-frame scares and tones down the gore in order to return to the feel of Carpenter's original. The scenes with Laurie and Michael are the most effective, and reach a satisfying conclusion when, after a climactic hair-raising chase she finally lops his head off. Atta girl! *Verdict:* 3/5

Urban Legend (1998)

Cast: Alicia Witt (Natalie), Jared Leto (Paul), Rebecca Gayheart (Brenda), Joshua Jackson (Damon), Natasha Gregson Wagner (Michelle Mancini), Loretta Devine (Reese), Tara Reid (Sasha), Michael Rosenbaum (Parker), Danielle Harris (Tosh), Robert Englund (Professor Wexler), John Neville (Dean Adams), Julian Richings (Janitor), Brad Dourif (Gas Station Attendant, uncredited)

Crew: Director Jamie Blanks, Producers Neal H Moritz & Gina Matthews & Michael McDonnell, Writer Silvio Horta, Cinematography James Cressanthis, Music Christopher Young, Editor Jay Cassidy, Production Designer Charles Breen, Special Make-Up Effects Martin Malivoire, 100 minutes

Story: A serial killer is at large on campus, murdering students in recreations of scenarios from urban legends. Natalie finds her friends, roommates and others are dropping like flies and tries to discover who might be doing such unspeakable things. Could it be Professor Wexler, the expert in urban legends? Could it be Parker, amoral journo for the college newspaper? Or could it be someone with a grudge against her for something in her past?

Background: A full-blooded throwback to the campus-based slashers of yore, with the necessary nods to *Scream* (and *Scream 2*), *Se7en* and *I Know What You Did Last Summer*, *Urban Legend* manages to serve up enough preposterous murders and decent scares to make it seem more than just a bandwagon jumper. The only slasher in this small-scale revival that did not have Kevin Williamson's name attached to it in one form or another, it had the sense to set up Englund as one of the major red herrings of the plot. Witt and Leto carry themselves through the necessary hoops with aplomb. While the urban legend theme runs out halfway through, it resurfaces at the climax for a suitably nasty conclusion. *Verdict:* 4/5

Ironically, the ongoing revival with tales of characters beleaguered by unwelcome psychos, also featured its very own unwelcome *Psycho* (1998). Directed by Gus Van Sant as a shot-for-shot remake and reusing Bernard Herrmann's original score, it was as much an attempt at cultural reappropriation as a pointless remake - its major achievement is to send you back to the original. The new cast are Vince Vaughan (a too-threatening Norman Bates), Anne Heche (Marion), Julianne Moore (Lila), Viggo Mortensen (a lunk-headed Sam Loomis) and William H Macy (Arbogast, the only spot-on performance). As if setting itself up for its own fall by following the script and camera set-ups (even to the point of recreating Hitchcock's stetson-wearing cameo) the film wilfully strikes wrong notes just when they will be most noticeable. Particularly perverse is the fact that, although updated to 90s America, no one mentions credit cards or has mobile phones yet at one point Lila says "I'll just get my Walkman." Another curious change is in the scene where the audience's gaze is aligned with Norman's voyeurism when Marion is showering. Here we also witness Norman masturbating which breaks the connection between us and him. We are suddenly distanced from him because of this and thus released from being implicated in his voyeurism. The possibility of reclaiming *Psycho* for a new audience unfamiliar with Hitchcock's original seems a fatuous reason for the project, given that the original is hardly a long-lost classic - rather it's a movie that continues to be quoted, referred to and generally ripped off in modern cinema. *Verdict:* 1/5 - for curiosity value alone

Scream 2 (1998)

Cast: David Arquette (Dwight 'Dewey' Riley), Neve Campbell (Sidney Prescott), Courtney Cox (Gale Weathers), Sarah Michelle Gellar (Casey 'CiCi' Cooper), Jamie Kennedy (Randy Meeks), Duane Martin (Joel, the Cameraman), Laurie Metcalf (Debbie Salt), Elise Neal (Hallie), Jerry O'Connell (Derek), Timothy Olyphant (Mickey), Jada Pinkett (Maureen Evans), Liev Schreiber (Cotton Weary), Lewis Arquette (Chief Lewis Hartley), Rebecca Gayheart (Sister Lois), Portia de Rossi

(Sister Murphy), Omar Epps (Phil Stevens), Tori Spelling (Sidney in *Stab*), Heather Graham (Casey in *Stab*), Kevin Williamson (Cotton's Interviewer)

Crew: Director Wes Craven, Producers Cathy Konrad & Marianne Maddalena, Writer Kevin Williamson, Cinematography Peter Deming, Music Marco Beltrami & Danny Elfman, Editor Patrick Lussier, Production Designer Bob Ziembicki, 120 minutes

Story: Now at university, Sidney Prescott is rebuilding her life after the Woodsboro murders, but the slaying of two fellow-students at the premiere of *Stab* - the film based on the killings, brings all the terror and old faces back. Gale Weathers arrives on campus to cover the slaying and is reunited with Dewey. Cotton Weary, now released from prison, surfaces in an attempt to get Sidney to do TV interviews with him. As the slaughter continues, Randy realises that someone is out to create a real-life sequel to the Woodsboro slayings which means more elaborate murders and a higher body count...

Background: "It's a classic case of life imitating art imitating life," says one less-clued-up character in *Scream 2*. Once again it's all about revenge, with Sidney's mother still haunting the proceedings because of her destruction of Billy Loomis' family life. Harking back to campus slashers such as *Splatter University* and *House On Sorority Row*, *Scream 2* manages to sustain its referentiality as well as the scares of the original whilst reuniting us with familiar faces. The plot both plays with sequel conventions (the body count is only slightly higher, none of the deaths are that much more elaborate) and film adaptations of 'real' events (Sidney's comment about Tori Spelling playing her in a movie comes true and *Stab* replays the opening scene of *Scream* in a craftily bog-standard slasher copy).

Memorable Lines: Randy: "When did she start smoking?" Dewey: "Just after those nude pictures of her on the internet." Gale: "It was just my head, it was Jennifer Aniston's body."

Verdict: 4/5

Scream 3 (1999)

Cast: David Arquette (Dwight 'Dewey' Riley), Neve Campbell (Sidney Prescott), Courtney Cox Arquette (Gale Weathers), Patrick Dempsey (Detective Mark Kincaid), Scott Foley (Roman Bridger), Lance Henriksen (John Milton), Matthew Keeslar (Tom Prinze), Jenny McCarthy (Sarah Darling/Tatum in *Stab 3*), Emily Mortimer (Angelina Tyler/Sidney in *Stab 3*), Parker Posey (Jennifer Jolie/Gale in *Stab 3*), Deon Richmond (Tyson Fox/Ricky in *Stab 3*), Carrie Fisher (Bianca Burnette), Liev Schreiber (Cotton Weary)

Crew: Director Wes Craven, Producers Cathy Konrad & Kevin Williamson & Marianne Maddalena, Writer Ehren Krueger, Cinematography Peter Deming, Music Marco Beltrami, Editor Patrick Lussier, Production Designer Bruce Alan Miller, 116 minutes

Story: Stab 3, another film based on the Woodsboro murders, is in production. Having changed her identity and moved to another part of America where she works as a phone crisis counsellor, Sidney Prescott is shocked to hear that Cotton Weary, now a television celebrity, has been murdered. A photograph of Sidney's mother, left at the scene of Weary's death suggests that someone is after her. Working as an adviser on the film, Dewey bumps into Gale once more and introduces her to the actors playing them in *Stab 3*. On the film set, the death of one of the actresses closes down production. The *Stab 3* cast, along with Sidney who emerges from hiding to help solve the case, start to fear for their lives. After all, if this is the final part in the trilogy of slayings, anyone could be next.

Background: Since Kevin Williamson was directing *Teaching Mrs Tingle*, scripting duties for *Scream 3* were given to Ehren Krueger, who had previously written the conspiracy thriller *Arlington Road* (1998). Williamson had written a treatment for the third and, we are led to believe, final instalment, but this was never used. Supposedly always planned as a trilogy, the cast are once again assembled, including Randy, who makes a touching video-return to explain the rules of the trilogy. Unfortunately, for all its threats, *Scream 3* never goes quite far enough. When Sidney asks Detective Kincaid what he knows about trilogies, his response that "All bets are off" implies that it's not just Cotton who's going to wind up dead this time. But by the end it's only the non-regulars who've bitten the dust, with Sidney, Dewey and Gale drifting off to a better life. Once again, it's the sins of the mother that return to haunt Sidney and the others but it almost feels like one sin too far, even though it just about ties up the entire trilogy. The best moments are mainly incidental, such as Carrie Fisher's bitter Carrie Fisher lookalike who didn't get the job in *Star Wars* because she wouldn't sleep with George Lucas, and Parker Posey's Gale Weathers constantly sniping at her real-life counterpart. Craven orchestrates the bloody proceedings well but the killer is too predictable this time and despite the thrills and the in-jokes (Roger Corman, and Kevin Smith's uber-slackers, Jay and Silent Bob, have cameos) there is a sense of going through the motions about the whole thing.

After this, Wes Craven directed his long-planned non-genre picture *Music Of The Heart*, which he hoped would finally dispel his label as a horror-movie director. Starring Meryl Streep and telling of a music teacher working with the kids in the Harlem ghetto, it was not a success. His next announced project was *Dracula 2000*. Old labels die hard.

Memorable Lines: 1) Cotton: "How do you know I've got a girl-friend?" Killer: "Because I'm right outside her bathroom door." 2) Sarah, to the Director: "I'm not happy that I'm 35 playing a 21-year-old; I'm not happy I have to die naked and I'm not happy that my character is too stupid to have a gun in the house even after her boyfriend's been cut into fish sticks!"

Verdict: 3/5

Scream 3 seemed to finally play out the brief revival of the slasher genre but echoes remain. *American Psycho*, directed by Mary Harron and starring Christian Bale as Jason Bateman, is a darkly comic adaptation of Bret Easton Ellis' 'unfilmable' novel (a troubled project originally linked to David Cronenberg and to star Leonardo DiCaprio). Playing down the book's grotesque violence and playing up the real horrors of 80s excess, Bateman still gets to chase someone with a chainsaw. Meanwhile, elements of the slasher continue to live on. The hugely successful docufake horror *The Blair Witch Project* conjures up the spirits of *Friday The 13th*, *The Texas Chainsaw Massacre* and *A Nightmare On Elm Street* with its tale of a documentary crew lost deep in the woods, tracked by unseen forces which might be the legendary Blair Witch, but could equally be the spirit of a long-executed child murderer. Needless to say, it all ends badly in a derelict house, deep in the forest. There is also box-office hit *Final Destination* where a group of teens narrowly escape a plane crash only to have their fates catching up with them through well-engineered 'natural' accidents. This is a slasher movie at heart, only the slasher in this case is Death itself.

These reworkings of the genre have proved hugely popular. One reason may be that this time there is no physical threat to do battle with. The teens are clueless as to what they are supposed to confront in order to stop the onslaught, which leaves the audiences uncertain as to the outcome.

More recently TV has embraced the slasher ethos, Chris Carter's short-lived *Millennium* involved Lance Henricksen's ultra-empathic serial-killer profiler Frank Black in a weekly trudge through the pitch-black underworld, seeking out maniacs with weird MOs. The problem was that Black was so empathic he virtually knew who the killer was before the opening credits had finished rolling, leaving little of interest for viewers to get involved with. In *Buffy The Vampire Slayer*, Sarah Michelle Gellar, who came to a bad end in both of her slasher-movie appearances (*I Know What You Did Last Summer* and *Scream 2*), is the embodiment of the 'final girl.' The show constantly mixes genre references: Buffy's friends are a mixture of old-world horror sensibilities (Giles, her 'watcher,' a studious Englishman whose knowledge and library of occult matters rival those of Van Helsing) and new-world/new-age pop culture (hormone-driven but occasionally courageous Xander, studious techno-wiz/witch Willow) who frequently refer to themselves as members of 'the Scooby gang,' Buffy is most often left to destroy evil by herself, armed with their advice and knowledge. An example of the show's influences is demonstrated in the episode 'Killed By Death.' In it, a demon not dissimilar in appearance to Fred Krueger stalks the hospital where Buffy is a patient. The demon, known as Der Kindestod (literally 'child death') is only seen by the children quarantined in the flu ward. Unsurprisingly, no grown-up believes them or Buffy, who sees him when in the grip of fever.

There are signs that the genre has a future. Ridley Scott will direct the screen adaptation of *Hannibal*, Thomas Harris' preposterous, studio-baiting sequel to *The Silence Of The Lambs*, with Julianne Moore as Clarice and Anthony Hopkins reprising his role as Hannibal Lecter. Although Michael Myers is now decapitated and Leatherface touring the East Coast doing Divine impressions, it's rumoured that Sean S Cunningham and New Line plan to revive everyone's favourite hockey-masked maniac in *Jason X*. This could be the Voorhees/Krueger showdown we all (haven't) been waiting for. An added feature is the possible casting of David Cronenberg. Just as long as it's got some really dim teenagers in it as well. And a cat.

9. Quick Slashers

It would be nearly impossible to provide an exhaustive list of the slasher movies that have been produced. It's also hard to draw a line between actual 'slashers' and movies that also portray psychopathic killers and their crimes (films such as Peter Bogdanovich's *Targets* (1968) or many of the 90s trend of serial killer vs. cop movies, for example). So here is a further list of movies that contain elements of the slasher movie in one form or another, should you wish to venture further...

American Gothic (1987, aka Hide And Go Shriek)
Director John Hough. Cast: Rod Steiger, Sarah Torgov, Yvonne De Carlo, Michael J Pollard, William Hootkins

Teenagers stranded on a small island get picked off by patriarch Steiger and his loopy brood before fighting back. Although entertaining at the start, it soon degenerates, becoming another running-through-the-woods movie. The scenery-chewing villains give the film an air of *The*

Hills Have Eyes adapted as an episode of *The Munsters*. De Carlo's inclusion doesn't help this comparison. *Verdict:* 2/5

Appointment With Fear (1985)

Director Alan Smithee (Ramzi Thomas). Cast: Michelle Little, Michael Wyle, Kerry Remsen, Doug Rowe

Produced by Moustapha Akaad, who was involved with the sequelisation of *Halloween*. This grafts the psychic vengeance theme of *Psychic Killer* (1974) onto the standard slasher plot to no great effect. It remains a matter of conjecture why director Thomas felt aggrieved enough to adopt the Smithee credit. *Verdict:* 2/5

April Fool's Day (1986)

Director Fred Walton. Cast: Jay Baker, Deborah Foreman, Deborah Goodrich, Ken Olandt, Amy Steel

Heiress Foreman invites her college friends to an April Fool's party at her family pile and the practical jokes soon turn into something nastier as various guests wind up dead. Or, rather they don't, as the whole thing is revealed to be a huge April Fool's joke. Even Foreman's insane twin sister was just Foreman all along. As irritating as it sounds. *Verdict:* 1/5

Bad Dreams (1988)

Director Andrew Fleming. Cast: Jennifer Rubin, Bruce Abbott, Richard Lynch, Dean Cameron

Another big cheat of a movie with Rubin playing the sole survivor of a Jonestown-style massacre awakening in hospital after a long coma and believing her cult leader (played by that great screen villain Lynch) is returning through her dreams to track her down à la *A Nightmare On Elm Street*. Various patients die before it is revealed to be a drug experiment by deranged psychiatrists. *Verdict:* 2/5

Bloodmoon (1991)

Director Alec Mills. Cast: Leon Lissek, Christine Amor, Ian Williams, Helen Thomson

Weary and belated Australian *Prom Night* rip-off, as Lissek's unhinged teacher stalks lover's lane garrotting couples with barbed wire. Even then, it's still not as entertaining as it sounds. *Verdict:* 1/5

Bloody Birthday (1980)

Director Ed Hunt. Cast: Susan Strasberg, Jose Ferrer, Lori Lethin, K C Martel, Elizabeth Hoy, Billy Jacoby, Andy Freeman

The Bad Seed (1958) times three meets the slashers uptown, as a trio of little horrors, all born during a solar eclipse, start whacking various members of the cast. No one believes the nice kid (Martel) and, because the villains are children, their exits are less than satisfying. *Verdict:* 2/5

The Boogeyman (1980, aka The Bogey Man)

Director Ulli Lommel. Cast: Suzanna Love, Ron James, John Carradine, Nicholas Love

First Hollywood movie from the director of the excellent *The Tenderness Of Wolves* (1973), this is a far more haphazard affair, with echoes of *Halloween* as well as Hans Christian Anderson's *The Snow Queen*. However, it does make a serious attempt to depart from standard slasher fare and contains some genuinely odd moments. The sequel, unsurprisingly called *Boogeyman II* (1982), is more an acidic commentary of working inside the Hollywood machine than a slasher sequel but, strangely, it remains banned in the UK. *Verdict:* 3/5

Cape Fear (1991)

Director Martin Scorsese. Cast: Robert De Niro, Nick Nolte, Jessica Lange, Juliette Lewis

A big-budget remake of the critically-lambasted original which pitted Robert Mitchum against Gregory Peck (both of whom have cameos in this version). Scorsese racks up the tension in this tale of psychotic ex-con out for vengeance against the lawyer who put him away. De Niro plays Max Cady as panto-psycho but his presence is undeniably threatening. The film also includes a fine *Friday The 13th* ending. *Verdict:* 4/5

Child's Play (1988)

Director Tom Holland. Cast: Catherine Hicks, Chris Sarandon, Alex Vincent, Brad Dourif

Like a slasher movie as imagined by Charles Band, the film that introduced the public to Chucky, the Good Guy doll possessed by the spirit of Charles Lee Ray, the Lakeside Strangler (Brad Dourif). Much terrorising ensues as Chucky attempts to possess the body of Hicks' son (Vincent) and to avenge Lee Ray's death. Efficient rather than enjoyable, the film spawned two proper sequels in 1990 and 1991 before being given the *Scream* postmodern make-over with *Bride Of Chucky* (1998). *Child's Play 3* became notorious in the UK after is was held responsible by the tabloid press for inspiring the murder of James Bulger by two older children, although whether they actually watched the film remains questionable. *Verdict:* 3/5, 2/5, 3/5, 4/5

Curtains (1982)

Director Jonathan Stryker (Richard Ciupka). Cast: Samantha Eggar, John Vernon, Linda Thorson, Maury Chaykin

Pretentious and tiresome slasher (the director in the movie bears the same name as the pseudonymous director of the movie) which borrows heavily from Sam Fuller's *Shock Corridor* (1963) in its tale of an actress

(Eggar) who pretends to be insane to experience genuine insanity in an asylum. Escaping to attend an audition session at an isolated house, she soon finds all other contenders are being killed by a masked killer. Despite the plot possibilities, the film remains painfully slow and annoyingly wordy. *Verdict:* 2/5

Dangerous Games (1988)

Director Stephen Hopkins. Cast: Miles Buchanan, Marcus Graham, Steven Grives, Sandy Lillingstone

A surprisingly effective slasher as a cop (Grives), fired for persecuting his superior's son (Buchanan) follows the boy and his friends as they break into a department store. Accidentally killing one of them, he adopts a 'slash and burn' policy to free himself and the film portrays the running battle between the increasingly deranged cop and the desperate teens. Stealing freely from *The Initiation* (1984) and William Lustig's *Maniac Cop* (1988), *Dangerous Games* took director Hopkins from Australia to direct *A Nightmare On Elm Street 3*. *Verdict:* 4/5

Dead Kids (1981, aka Strange Behaviour, Small-Town Massacre)

Director Michael Laughlin. Cast: Michael Murphy, Louise Fletcher, Dan Shor, Fiona Lewis, Arthur Dignam

Teen slasher oddity made in New Zealand with more plot than most, concerning a psychiatrist who primes his patients to go out and kill those who oppose him. Unfortunately, he's no expert in patient-therapist relationships and telling one of them to "Go and kill your father" backfires in a satisfyingly twisted conclusion. *Verdict:* 3/5

Das Deutsche Kettensägenmassaker (1991, aka The German Chainsaw Massacre)

Director Christoph Schlingensief. Cast: Karina Fallenstein, Suzanne Bredehöft, Artur Albrecht

Both amateurish and pretentious slasher movie set just after German reunification, featuring a deranged capitalist family intent on turning their less well-off East German counterparts into frankfurters. Heavy-handed satire that, while only 63 minutes long, still outstays its welcome. *Verdict:* 0/5

Dreamhouse (1981)

Director Al Beresford. Cast: Ian Saynor, Yvonne Nicholson, Orla Pederson, Brian Croucher, Robert Dorning

With a screenplay by horror regular Michael Armstrong and produced by Stanley Long (the uncredited cinematographer on *Repulsion* (1965)), this 55-minute, effective slasher short was released as a support for vigilante gore-fest *The Exterminator* (1981). A young couple move into a new house only for the wife to be plagued by visions of bloody murder by a razor-wielding maniac. She's convinced that the house is haunted. But it's far worse, she's precognitive and it's all about to happen... *Verdict:* 4/5

The Driller Killer (1979)

Director Abel Ferrara. Cast: Jimmy Laine (Ferrara), Carolyn Marz, Harry Schultz, Baybi Day

Borderline slasher which comes across as a low-rent tribute to Polanski's *Repulsion*. NY artist Laine is driven insane by the punk rock band upstairs, his junkie girlfriend and the daily visions of the winos on the streets, in whom he sees his future if he is unable to overcome his artist's block. Arming himself with a power drill he sets out to try and correct the balance of his life. Intense debut from Ferrara which was the *cause célèbre* of the UK 'video nasty' debate of 1984. Now re-released on video in a fuller dramatic version but with scenes of violence trimmed from the original Vipco release. *Verdict:* 4/5

Frightmare (1974)

Director Pete Walker. Cast: Rupert Davies, Sheila Keith, Deborah Fairfax, Paul Greenwood, Kim Butcher

The British version of *Texas Chainsaw Massacre*, complete with grotty bedsits, lock-ups and fake psychics. Keith is the dotty matriarch whose taste for human flesh is concealed by her doting husband (Davies), but which doesn't stay suppressed for long and neither does the use of power tools. The best of Walker's films, borne from his troubled partnership with writer David McGillivray, this lacks the all-consuming holocaust presented by Hooper's film but, along with *The Wicker Man* (1973) and *Death Line* (1972), *Frightmare* remains one of the last impressive horror films made in the UK. That's Andrew Sachs getting killed at the beginning, by the way. *Verdict:* 4/5

Funny Man (1994)

Director Simon Sprackling. Cast: Tim James, Christopher Lee, Benny Young, Matthew Devitt, Rhona Cameron

Oh, dear God, no. Along with *The Return Of The Texas Chainsaw Massacre* (also 1994), this marks the utter nadir of the slasher. An evil jester (James) kills various stereotypes (including a Scooby-Doo Velma lookalike) in unamusing ways, wisecracking as he does so. Devoid of any imagination, plotting or conflict, it's basically *Carry On Elm Street*. Even worse is that I can still remember the theme song after all these years. *Verdict:* 0/5

Hide And Go Shriek (1987, aka Close Your Eyes And Pray)

Director Skip Schoolnik. Cast: George Thomas, Donna Baltron, Brittain Frye, Annette Sinclair

A group of kids hold an all-night party at a deserted department store (see *The Initiation*) and are butchered by a killer in drag (see *Terror Train*). Other than play spot-the-slasher-references this really has very little going for it. *Verdict:* 1/5

The Horror Show (1989, aka House III - The Horror Show)

Director James Isaacs. Cast: Lance Henriksen, Brion James, Rita Taggart, Deedee Pfeiffer

Originally scheduled to be part of Sean S Cunningham's comedy-horror *House* series, he ruled it to be too dark for inclusion (although the UK video release included the connection). Telling the tale of Max Jenke (the ever-villainous James) who, upon execution, returns as electrical energy to get his revenge on the cop who caught him (Henriksen) and his family. Pre-empting Wes Craven's *Shocker*, this is a grim little movie with good performances all round and a reasonable pace. It remains gripping viewing despite the behind-the-scenes upheaval of the firing of the original director, New Zealander David Blyth, and his replacement with special effects man Isaacs. Blyth went on to direct the interesting vampire movie *Red Blooded American Girl* (1991). *Verdict:* 3/5

The Initiation (1984)

Director Larry Stewart. Cast: Daphne Zuniga, Vera Miles, Clu Gulager, James Read, Marilyn Kagan

Sorority pledge Zuniga (her movie debut) has enough troubles breaking into her father's department store as part of her college hazing ritual without having to worry about escaped lunatics and flashbacks masquerading as nightmares. One of the escapees turns out to be her real father, put in the asylum by Miles and Gulager so that they could marry. Who is really killing off everyone else during the night? Surely not someone's evil twin sister who nobody knew about until the film's climax? Surely not! *Verdict:* 2/5

Intruder (1988)

Director Scott Spiegel. Cast: Elizabeth Cox, Renée Estevez, Danny Hicks, David Byrnes, Sam Raimi, Bruce Campbell, Ted Raimi

A group of supermarket night-shift workers fall victim to the vengeance of one of the employee's psychotic ex-boyfriends in this extremely gory (although not in the UK version) and stylishly shot, late addition to the slasher cycle. Director Spiegel previously co-wrote *Evil*

Dead 2 (1987), not that you'd know it from this surprise-free effort if it wasn't for Campbell's and the Raimi brothers' presence. *Verdict:* 2/5

Killer's Moon (1978)

Director Alan Birkinshaw. Cast: Anthony Forrest, Tom Marshall, Georgina Kean, Nigel Gregory

Incompetent and mainly pseudonymously-made slasher involving four escaped maniacs and a busload of schoolgirls to monotonously violent effect. Cannot even lay claim to best horror film made in the Lake District (that honour goes to Jorge Grau's *The Living Dead At The Manchester Morgue* (1974)). *Verdict:* 1/5

Lady, Stay Dead (1982)

Director Terry Bourke. Cast: Chard Hayward, Louise Howitt, Deborah Coulls, Roger Ward

Meaningless title, pointless film as psycho-gardener (another one? see below) Hayward attacks and kills his female employers to overcome his sexual inadequacies. Woefully uninteresting. *Verdict:* 1/5

The Love Butcher (1975)

Director Mikel Angel. Cast: Erik Stern, Kay Neer, Jeremiah Beecher, Edward Roehm, Robin Sherwood

Only released in 1982, this tale of a crippled gardener who reverts to his virile *alter ego* brother in order to seduce and kill the women who have mistreated him, predates the slasher boom. It comes with ridiculously overwrought dialogue and self-conscious slow-motion scenes, as well as the use of a lawnmower as a murder weapon (later used in the intentional slasher-spoof *Wacko!* (1982). *Verdict:* 3/5

Mil Gritos Tiene La Noche (1981, aka Pieces)

Director Juan Piquer Simon. Cast: Christopher George, Edmund Purdom, Lynda Day George, Paul L Smith

Hackneyed and misogynistic Spanish slasher involving a killer loose on campus who is collecting female body parts to build his own woman (it all dates back to some childhood trauma involving a pornographic jigsaw - honest). Smith (Bluto in Robert Altman's *Popeye* (1980)) is the main suspect, being large, lecherous and bearded but the killer is as obvious as the GI in *The Prowler*. The highlight of this extraordinarily bloody film is the scene where the killer lurks in a lift, attempting to hide a chainsaw behind his back. *Verdict:* 2/5

Motel Hell (1980)

Director Kevin Connor. Cast: Rory Calhoun, Paul Linke, Nancy Parsons, Nina Axelrod, Wolfman Jack

Along with *Return To Horror High*, this remains the high point of slasher introspection until *Scream*. Gleefully inflating *The Texas Chainsaw Massacre*'s roadside human barbecue to a state-wide business concession ('It takes all kinds of critters to make Farmer Vincent's fritters!'), the acting, script and pace are top-notch. Full of sick jokes at the expense of both pop culture and horror movies. The *grand guignol* climax where Calhoun, wearing a pig's head, duels to the death with Linke with chainsaws in a slaughterhouse while Axelrod slides inexorably towards a circular saw is one of the outstanding moments from the slashers. *Verdict:* 5/5

Mother's Day (1980)

Director Charles Kaufman. Cast: Nancy Hendrickson, Deborah Luce, Tania Pierce, Holden McGuire

Another anniversary slasher, this retains enough black comedy to be worth watching by virtue of its murderous family driven insane by modern life's endless stream of pop culture. And, in a 'by the sword' fashion, they are duly disposed of in fitting fashion (radio antennae, electric carving knife, TV set, etc.). Sadly, despite its merits, it remains banned in the UK. *Verdict:* 4/5

Nail-Gun Massacre (1985)

Directors: Terry Lofton & Bill Leslie. Cast: Rocky Patterson, Michelle Meyer, Ron Queen

Following a rape committed by a bunch of construction workers, the perpetrators and various other Texan extras are disposed of by a motorcycle-helmeted killer with the eponymous tool. While another implement movie might sound entertaining, this one is sadly low on everything except nails. *Verdict:* 1/5

Nightwatch (1994)

Director Ole Bornedal. Cast: Nikolaj Waldau, Sofie Graaboel, Kim Bodnia, Lotte Andersen, Ulf Pilgaard

Excellent teens-in-peril movie revolving around Waldau's job as night watchman at the local mortuary, the increasingly sadistic dares between him and his best friend, and a vicious killer who targets prostitutes. Bornedal keeps the tension high until the climax, when it becomes almost unbearable. As with George Sluzier's *The Vanishing* (1988), Bornedal remade *Nightwatch* for Hollywood, with Ewan Macgregor and Nick

Nolte in Waldau and Pilgaard's roles respectively and, like *The Vanishing* (1992), it was dreadful. *Verdict:* 4/5

Nightmares In A Damaged Brain (1981, aka Nightmare)

Director Romano Scavolini. Cast: Baird Stafford, Sharon Smith, C J Cooke, Mik Cribben, Danny Ronen

A schizophrenic who, as a child, murdered his parents, is released from an asylum and picks up the slaughtering where he left off. This gory, derivative and thoroughly dreary psycho-killer movie has little to recommend it other than the endless arguments over who actually did the special make-up effects and the fact that its UK distributor was jailed for six months under the draconian 'video nasty' bill of 1984 after releasing a print containing 60 seconds of censored material. *Verdict:* 1/5

One By One (1987, aka The Majorettes)

Director Bill Hinzman. Cast: Kevin Kindlin, Terrie Godfrey, Mark V Jevicky, Russ Streiner, John Russo

Russo, who wrote *Night Of The Living Dead* (1968), here provides an exceptionally twisted plot involving a murderous sheriff, a local peeping Tom, various cheerleading bimbos, extortion and contract killing which lifts this film out of the standard slasher quagmire. Unfortunately, like Russo's previous *Midnight* (1981), it is also exceptionally depressing viewing, providing not a single sympathetic character as well as suffering from bad acting and lacklustre direction. *Verdict:* 1/5

Open House (1987, aka Multiple Listings)

Director Jag Mudhra. Cast: Joseph Bottoms, Adrienne Barbeau, Rudy Ramos, Mary Stavin

Barbeau plays a realtor whose colleagues are lured to addresses and slaughtered by a homeless vagrant before she finally confronts him. This predictable slasher soon disposes the interesting 'haves and have-nots' class angle in favour of the usual cheap shocks, including another reprise of the 'he's in the house' phone call business from *Black Christmas*. *Verdict:* 2/5

Popcorn (1991)

Directors: Mark Herrier & Alan Ormsby. Cast: Jill Schoelen, Tom Villard, Dee Wallace Stone, Derek Rydall, Ray Walston, Tony Roberts

Students aim to save their cash-strapped film department by holding an all-night horror film festival at a local cinema. Schoelen is the heroine whose flashbacks to a 60s Kenneth Anger-style underground film massacre are vital to the uncovering of a Dr Phibes-style killer. The killer uses the spoof movies' William Castle-style gimmicks to murder various cast members. This rickety but thoroughly enjoyable throwback, despite its shortcomings, has enough charm and good humour to keep it ticking over. Any film whose climax involves death by giant rubber mosquito is always welcome. *Verdict:* 3/5

Raising Cain (1992)

Director Brian De Palma. Cast: John Lithgow, Lolita Davidovich, Steve Bauer, Frances Sternhagen, Gregg Henry

De Palma's version of *Peeping Tom* leaves aside questions of audience scopophilia and goes for suspense and blackly-comic moments, with Lithgow enjoying multiple roles as the unhinged child psychologist kidnapping children to reproduce the experiments that his equally mad psychologist father (Lithgow) carried out on him during childhood. Meanwhile his imaginary twin, Cain (Lithgow), pushes him ever closer to murder. Throwing references to *Psycho* and *Tenebrae* with careless abandon, this hugely entertaining movie feels like a two-fingered air-clearing of *homages* before De Palma returned with the superior gangster movie *Carlito's Way* (1993). *Verdict:* 4/5

The Redeemer (1976)

Director Constantine S Goochis. Cast: Michael Hollingsworth, Damien Knight, Gyr Patterson, Nikki Barthen, T G Finkbinder

A group of people are invited to a spurious high school reunion where they are lectured by the killer about being punished for their 'sins' before being violently dispatched. Worryingly, the only 'sins' which are shown to have been committed are by two of the women and these are being gay and being sexually active. While Jason, Freddy and Michael might have had their moral agendas, the killer of this nasty little tale appears to be some kind of religious emissary and the film-makers come across as reactionary bigots. *Verdict:* 1/5

Return Of The Family Man (1989)

Director John Murlowski. Cast: Ron Smerczak, Liam Cundill, Terence Reis, Debra Kaye

Made in South Africa but set in an indeterminate part of America, Smerczak plays the escaped maniac who keeps his murdered family mummified in his dilapidated mansion. Cue a group of teenagers who have mistakenly rented said mansion for the holidays... Much running around and dying ensues to no great effect. *Verdict:* 1/5

Rush Week (1989)

Director Bob Bralver. Cast: Dean Hamilton, Pamela Ludwig, Roy Thinnes, Courtney Gebhart

Unusually featuring an undercover cop pretending to be a student in order to flush out a crazed axe murderer, this tired collegiate slasher missed the boat by nearly ten years and can barely be bothered to plant the requisite red herrings to divert our attention away from the fact that the killer is obviously the misery-guts dean (Thinnes). *Verdict:* 2/5

Savage Weekend (1976, aka The Killer Behind The Mask)
Director David Paulsen. Cast: Christopher Allport, James Doerr, Marilyn Hamlin, Kathleen Heaney, David Gale

A group of friends visit a remote country house for a dirty weekend and are dispatched by a maniac with a variety of domestic implements. Remaining on the shelf until 1981, the full-length version of this *Friday The 13th* precursor involved as many sexual couplings as killings. So much so that the killer's presence feels like an afterthought. *Verdict:* 2/5

The Scaremaker (1982)
Director Robert Deubel. Cast: Julie Montgomery, James Carroll, Hal Holbrook

Little to recommend this collegiate slasher, set during a fancy dress party, other than Holbrook's appearance. Not that he looks like he wants to be there either. *Verdict:* 1/5

Schizo (1976)
Director Pete Walker. Cast: Lynne Frederick, John Leyton, Stephanie Beacham, John Fraser, Jack Watson, Queenie Watts

Walker, one of Britain's most notable exploitation directors, produced three interestingly grim movies (*House of Whipcord* (1974), *Frightmare* and *House of Mortal Sin* (1975)) with writer David McGillivray. Their temperamental relationship and their luck ended with *Schizo*, which tells of Frederick's persecution by a mad slasher who turns out to be... Frederick. Red herring-laden and plodding, the disinterest McGillivray had for the project is reflected on screen as the clichés pour out. The film's slogan 'When the left hand doesn't know what the right hand is doing' was pulled after complaints from mental health agencies. *Verdict:* 1/5

Schizoid (1980)
Director David Paulsen. Cast: Klaus Kinski, Mariana Hill, Craig Wasson, Flo Gerrish, Christopher Lloyd

As members of a therapy group are picked off by a particularly vicious killer, one of the patients, a newspaper columnist, decides to investigate. As with non-slasher horror pics *Titan Find* and *Crawlspace*, Kinski's barn-storming performance as the group's doctor is the only reason to watch this mediocre nonsense. *Verdict:* 2/5

Shocker (1989)
Director Wes Craven. Cast: Mitch Pileggi, Peter Berg, Cami Cooper, Michael Murphy, Timothy Leary, Alice Cooper, Theodore Raimi, Heather Langenkamp

Having lost the *Elm Street* franchise, Craven attempted to kick-start another with this tale of demented family-slaughtering TV-repairman Horace Pinker (Pileggi, later to become a household name as Assistant Director Skinner in *The X-Files*) who returns after his execution via dreams and TV signals to wreak revenge on his estranged son who shopped him to the cops. Nowhere near as entertaining as it sounds, Pinker remains a third-rate Freddy Krueger wannabe, down to the poor one-liners as he dispatches his victims. *Verdict:* 2/5

Silent Scream (1980)

Director Denny Harris. Cast: Rebecca Balding, Cameron Mitchell, Avery Schreiber, Barbara Steele, Brad Reardon, Yvonne De Carlo

More mad-family goings-on as Balding and three friends miss out on college housing and rent rooms at De Carlo's old dark house. Above-average fare given its low body count, with strong performances and atmospheric scenes. *Silent Scream* also benefits from genre-favourite Steele as the mad daughter and a seat-clutching climax. *Verdict:* 3/5

Sisters (1973, aka Blood Sisters)

Director Brian De Palma. Cast: Margot Kidder, Jennifer Salt, William Finley, Charles Durning

De Palma's first psycho-thriller remains one of his best, reworking *Psycho* in a tale of Kidder who, when approached by men, is possessed by the personality of her dead Siamese twin and promptly stabs them to death. As well as a genuinely disturbing hallucination sequence *Sisters* is, like Richard Fleischer's *The Boston Strangler* (1968), one of those rare films that uses split screens to inventive narrative effect. *Verdict:* 4/5

Slaughter High (1987, aka April Fool's Day)

Directors: Peter Litten & George Dugdale & Mark Ezra. Cast: Caroline Munro, Simon Scuddamore, Carmin Iannaccone, Donna Yeager

Gruesome deaths at a high school reunion turn out to be revenge slayings by a deranged nerd, horribly disfigured after his classmates' prank backfired. Made in the UK with everyone sporting cod-American accents. The three directors content themselves with ripping off *Terror Train*, *The Redeemer* and *The Burning* while the end (the victims returning as ghosts to pop out the murderer's eyes) is lifted from *Maniac*. *Verdict:* 1/5

Slaughterhouse (1988)

Director Rick Roessler. Cast: Sherry Bendorf, Don Barrett, William Houck, Joe Barton, Jane Higginson

Another dispiriting *Texas Chainsaw Massacre* copy, with chunky maniac Barton breaking from killing teens long enough to help kill off the meat marketers who are ruining his father's slaughterhouse business. *Verdict:* 1/5

The Slayer (1981)

Director J S Cardone. Cast: Sarah Kendall, Frederick Flynn, Carol Kottenbrook, Alan McRae, Michael Holmes

A rather nasty beastie haunts Kay's (Kendall) dreams and when she and her husband, along with two friends, go to a holiday island, she recognises the place immediately... Butchery ensues with some enjoyably tense moments and a twist ending that for once doesn't disappoint. *Verdict:* 3/5

Sorority House Massacre (1986)

Director Carol Frank. Cast: Angela O'Neill, Wendy Martel, Pamela Ross, John C Russell

Having witnessed her entire family being slaughtered, sorority pledge O'Neill suffers flashbacks which link her to the killer (Russell), who promptly escapes from the asylum to pursue her and her under-clothed sorority sisters in this hackneyed *Halloween* retread. *Verdict:* 1/5

Stage Fright (1987, aka Deliria, Bloody Bird, Aquarius)

Director Michele Soavi. Cast: David Brandon, Barbara Cupisti, Roberto Gugorov, Giovanni Lombardo Radice

A dance company working on a production of the Jack the Ripper story are terrorised by an owl-mask-wearing maniac. Soavi, a protégé of Dario Argento, debuted with this demented mid-Atlantic-dubbed slasher which contains some effective set pieces, not least the climax which involves a bit of business with a key, a chainsaw and much carnage. *Verdict:* 3/5

Sweet Sixteen (1982)

Director Jim Sotos. Cast: Bo Hopkins, Susan Strasberg, Aleisa Shirley, Dana Kimmell, Don Stroud, Patrick Macnee, Michael Pataki, Sharon Farrell

Poor Melissa's (Shirley) boyfriends have a nasty habit of ending up dead, but who is killing them? This unatmospheric slasher puts its vaguely starry cast through wooden dialogue, red herrings galore and a tired old dead-twin-sister revelation whilst retaining a dubious interest in Melissa's naked body, which Sotos attempts to work into the film every 15 minutes or so. *Verdict:* 1/5

Tenebrae (1982, aka Unsane)

Director Dario Argento. Cast: Anthony Franciosa, John Saxon, Guiliano Gemma, Daria Nicolodi, John Steiner

After the gothic excesses of *Suspiria* and *Inferno*, Argento's next film, while still strictly a *giallo*, also pulls back in everything that the slasher genre took from his movies (glamorous women being gruesomely murdered, stylishly gory set pieces, shoals of red herrings) and gives it all a good stir in this tale of Franciosa's crime-novelist's PR junket to launch his new book being plagued by a series of vicious killings. While the whodunit revelations may not overtax the jaded viewer, the film's visual pyrotechnics and its knowing humour definitely make it a cut above its US competitors. *Verdict:* 5/5

Terror At Tenkiller (1987)

Director Ken Meyer. Cast: Mike Wiles, Stacey Logan, Michele Merchant, Dale Buckmaster

Tired and amateurish *Friday The 13th* clone with Logan terrorised by a deranged handyman at an isolated lakeside campsite. He even leaps out of the lake to grab her at the finale. Ho hum. *Verdict:* 1/5

The Toolbox Murders (1978)

Director Dennis Donnelly. Cast: Cameron Mitchell, Pamelyn Ferdin, Wesley Eure, Nicolas Beauvy

'What he does to your nerves is almost as frightening as what he does to his victims!' yells the poster tagline for this misogynist nonsense about a psychotic handyman (Mitchell) who blames the death of his daughter on the loose morals of modern women. Lensed by Gary Graver, a one-time cameraman for Orson Welles, the first cut allegedly contained hardcore porn sequences, which would be the only way to make it more offensive. Mitchell increases the horror by singing to his victims. The title explains the rest in this feeble attempt to remake Bava's *Sei Donne Per L'Assassino*. Currently re-released on video in the UK, I must admit I haven't had the heart to find out whether it has sustained further cuts or not. *Verdict:* 0/5

The Town That Dreaded Sundown (1977)

Director Charles B Pierce. Cast: Ben Johnson, Andrew Prine, Dawn Wells, Jimmy Clem

Retelling the 'true' story of the sadistic Phantom Killer who launched a reign of terror on Texarkana in 1946, Pierce, who also bored audiences with *The Evictors* (1979) and *The Legend Of Boggy Creek* (1972), piles on the sadistic teen killings whilst neglecting anything that might hold the audiences' interest. *Verdict:* 0/5

The Ugly (1996)

Director Scott Reynolds. Cast: Paolo Rotondo, Rebecca Hobbs, Roy Ward, Vanessa Byrnes

Mystifyingly praised on its release, this is a slight and tiring serial-killer-versus-psychiatrist movie with a lot of pretensions and little substance, made in New Zealand. With multiple stealings from *The Silence Of The Lambs* and *Henry: Portrait Of A Serial Killer* it finally gives up entirely and goes for the 'it's all a dream, or is it?' ending. *Verdict:* 1/5

When A Stranger Calls (1979)

Director Fred Walton. Cast: Carol Kane, Charles Durning, Tony Beckley

After losing her charges to the psychotic Beckley several years ago, baby-sitter Kane is stalked once more when he escapes from a nearby asylum. Opening with a competent staging of the classic urban legend, Kane is told that the threatening phone calls she has been receiving are coming from inside the house. The rest of the film remains uncertain whether to be a slasher movie, a vigilante movie or a cry for common sense concerning proper facilities for the mentally ill as Beckley, in a tragic rather than threatening performance, ends up sleeping rough on the streets. Spawned a 90s sequel, also starring Kane and Durning (Beckley, as well as being killed at the end of this one also died in real life), entitled *When a Stranger Calls Back. Verdict:* 4/5, 3/5

10. Hey, Wasn't That...?

A collection of famous faces from the slashers:

Jason Alexander - 'Dave' in *The Burning*. Amiable character who doesn't get killed, but dispenses irritating wisdom to other, more lovelorn characters and runs a black market in condoms. Best known since for his long-running role as the angst-ridden George Costanza in *Seinfeld*.

Patricia Arquette - 'Kristen' in *A Nightmare On Elm Street 3 - Dream Warriors*. Another of those girls who beat Freddy senseless (bravo). Best known since for her roles in *True Romance* and David Lynch's *Lost Highway*.

Kevin Bacon - 'Jack' in *Friday The 13th*. Not his first film (he'd already played a snooty frat boy in *National Lampoon's Animal House* the year before), but it's nice to see that at least one actor from this series had a career afterwards.

Dana Carvey - 'Assistant' in *Halloween II*, in a blink-and-you'll-miss-him left-profile as he gets sent off by a TV reporter to 'Get statements from the parents.' *Wayne's World*'s Garth.

George Clooney - 'Oliver' in *Return To Horror High*. Plays an actor on the movie *Horror High*, who gets a better offer and leaves the set. But who's that over there? Hello? Hello?

Jamie Lee Curtis - 'Laurie' in *Halloween*, 'Kim' in *Prom Night*, 'Alana' in *Terror Train*. The ultimate final girl. The slasher movie would never have been what it was without her (and that's meant in a nice way). Went on to star in *Trading Places, A Fish Called Wanda* and *True Lies*. Then came back to the slasher for *Halloween H20*. Now Lady Haden-Guest - which sounds like an entirely different kind of horror.

Johnny Depp - 'Glen Lantz' in *A Nightmare On Elm Street*. Looking about 12 with his amazing 80s hairstyle, Johnny gets sucked to his death in his own bed. Made a cameo reappearance in *Freddy's Dead - The Final Nightmare* in an anti-drug advert where Freddy clobbers him with a frying pan. Big yucks.

Crispin Glover - 'Jim' in *Friday The 13th - The Final Chapter*. Spends most of this film worrying about being a 'dead fuck' before asking the dumbest question ever asked in a slasher movie: "Where's the corkscrew?" Turned in the role of his career in 1987 as the jittery speed-addict in Tim Hunter's *River's Edge* and has since appeared in Jim Jarmusch's *Dead Man* and *The People Vs Larry Flynt*.

Daryl Hannah - plays an unhappy camper in *Campsite Massacre*. Fame beckoned the next year with *Blade Runner*.

Tom Hanks - 'Elliott' in *He Knows You're Alone*. Unfortunately, Tom survives the carnage, disappearing after his main scene where he attempts to psychoanalyse Amy on a trip to the fairground. Shame.

Holly Hunter - 'Camper' in *The Burning*. The *Friday The 13th* clone that produced talent by the ton, including this Oscar-winning actress' first performance. She gets out alive, smokes some cigarettes and utters the line, "But how are we gonna get out of here?"

Linnea Quigley - 'Dolores' in *Graduation Day*. Never exactly 'famous' but any genre film with her in usually results in a few moments of gratuitous nudity - including this one. Other fine celluloid moments include *Return Of The Living Dead*, *Night Of The Demons* and *Hollywood Chainsaw Hookers*.

George A Romero - The director of *Night Of The Living Dead* makes a small cameo as a policeman in *The Silence Of The Lambs*.

Fisher Stevens - 'Woodstock' in *The Burning* - weird character who giggles a lot. Gets hacked to bits on a raft, and his death got hacked to bits by the censors. Has since worked with John Sayles, Tim Robbins and appeared as the slightly offensive Asian professor in the *Short Circuit* movies.

Rachel Ward - Before *Dead Men Don't Wear Plaid* and *The Thorn Birds*, Ms Ward played the motorcycle-helmeted maniac in *Terror Eyes* and Daryl Hannah's fellow-camper in *Campsite Massacre*.

11. Reference Materials

Books

Men, Women And Chainsaws by Carol Clover, UK: bfi, 1992, Paperback, 260 pages, £9.99, ISBN 0861704190 Not merely a book to salve the conscience of the devoted slasher-movie fan but a valuable examination of aspects of gender in film and audience. In separate chapters, Clover analyses slasher movies, possession movies, rape-revenge films and the question of 'the look' in horror films.

Censored by Tom Dewe Mathews, UK: Chatto & Windus, 1994, Trade Paperback, 298 pages, £14.99, ISBN 0701138734 A history of the BBFC from the Cinematograph Act of 1909 to the present day. A fascinating and frightening study of the minds at work behind the scissors. Particularly useful are the sections on the travails of *The Texas Chainsaw Massacre*, *Henry: Portrait Of A Serial Killer* and the 'video nasty' debates.

Scream - The Unofficial Companion To The Scream Trilogy by John Brosnan, UK: Boxtree, 2000, Trade Paperback, 144 pages, £9.99, ISBN 0752271628 Entertaining knock-off for Wes Craven's postmodern slashers, includes credits, synopses, star biogs and sizeable interviews and career histories of Kevin Williamson and Wes Craven.

For One Week Only - The World Of Exploitation Films by Richard Meyers, US: New Century Publishers, 1983, Trade Paperback, 270 pages, $12.95, ISBN 0832901423 Long deleted, schizophrenic work divided into three chapters: Sex, Violence and Horror. Worth tracking down for the rarity of some of the films under scrutiny, but Meyers' habit of continually biting that hand that feeds the book (in much the same fashion as Michael Medved) begins to tire after a while.

The Aurum Film Encyclopedia: Horror edited by Phil Hardy, UK: Aurum Press, 1993, Hardcover, 496 pages, £30.00, ISBN 185410263X Monumental reference work, arranged chronologically and alphabetically, contains reviews and brief plot summaries of most horror films released since cinema began.

Sex, Stupidity And Greed - Inside The American Movie Industry by Ian Grey, US: Juno Books, 1997, Paperback, 240 pages, $15.95, ISBN 0965104273 Sardonic critical work on the Hollywood system, includes candid interviews with Wes Craven, John Waters and *Heathers* director Michael Lehmann, as well as the excellent article 'Life-Affirming Qualities of Extreme Gore.'

Alfred Hitchcock And The Making Of Psycho by Stephen Rebello, UK: Marion Boyars Publishers, 1990, Paperback, 224 pages, £12.95, ISBN 0714530034 The title says it all. Exhaustive work on the grandfather of slasher movies, detailing everything from pre- to post-production. Recommended.

Killing For Culture by David Kerekes & David Slater, UK: Annihilation Press, 1993, Paperback, 300 pages, £11.95, ISBN 1871592208 An intelligent book requiring strong nerves. Kerekes and Slater examine the myths surrounding 'snuff' movies, cinema's appropriation of the 'snuff' theme for its own ends and audience attitudes to both screen violence and documentaries featuring actual death footage.

Screen Violence edited by Karl French, UK: Bloomsbury Publishing, 1997, Paperback, 248 pages, £6.99, ISBN 0747530939 Well-reasoned arguments from all sides of the continuing debate about screen violence and its effects in one wide-ranging volume. Contributors include: Martin Amis, Mary Whitehouse, Kim Newman, Alexander Walker, Pauline Kael and Camille Paglia.

Slasher Movies On Video & DVD

While many of the 1980-82 slashers have long since been deleted, it's always worth having a dig through your local video library, particularly if it's a well-established one that has been hoarding films for years. Others, such as *Texas Chainsaw Massacre 2/3*, *The New York Ripper* and *Slumber Party Massacre 2/3* have been refused a certificate in the UK. Those that are still available include:

The Burning (1981) Vipco, VIP015, £11.99
Deranged (1974) Quantum Leap, EX101, £11.99
Fatal Attraction (1987) Paramount, VHR2293, £8.99, Widescreen w/ original ending VHR2685 £11.99
Friday The 13th (1980) Warner Terrorvision, SO11172, £7.99
Friday The 13th Part 2 (1981) Paramount, BRP4346, £7.99
Friday The 13th Part 3 (1982) Paramount, VHR2211, £7.99
Friday The 13th - The Final Chapter (1984) VHR2216, £7.99
Friday The 13th Part V - A New Beginning (1985) VHR2227, £7.99
Friday The 13th Part VI - Jason Lives (1986) VHR2236, £7.99

Friday The 13th Part VII - The New Blood (1988) VHR2300, £7.99

Friday The 13th Part VIII - Jason Takes Manhattan (1989) VHR2366, £7.99

Halloween (1978) - MIA, V3571, £7.99, Widescreen edition, MIA, V3453, £11.99

Halloween 2 (1981) MIA, V359208, £7.99

Halloween/Halloween 2 Double-bill tape, MIA, V3342, £11.99

Halloween 4 - The Return Of Michael Myers (1988) Digital Ent., DE9027, £7.99

Halloween 5 (1989) Digital Ent., DE9028, £7.99

Halloween - The Curse Of Michael Myers (1995) Cinema Club, CC7803, £11.99

Halloween H20 - Twenty Years Later (1998) Hollywood Pictures, D610888, £14.99

Hell Night (1981) MIA, V3335, £10.99

Henry: Portrait Of A Serial Killer (1987) 4-Front, 0541443, £5.99

I Know What You Did Last Summer (1997) Entertainment, EVS1252, £5.99, DVD, EDV9019, £12.99

I Still Know What You Did Last Summer (1998) Columbia Tristar, CVR28060, £10.99, DVD, CDR98060, £14.99

A Nightmare On Elm Street (1985) Entertainment, EVS1293, £7.99

A Nightmare On Elm Street Part 2 - Freddy's Revenge (1986) Entertainment, EVS, £7.99

A Nightmare On Elm Street Part 3 - Dream Warriors (1987) Entertainment, EVS, £7.99

· (These three titles also available as a box set EVS1296, all other *Elm Street* titles are currently deleted)

Peeping Tom (1960) Warner, SO38187, £10.99

Pranks (1982, aka *The Dorm That Dripped Blood*) VPD468, £8.99

Prom Night (1980) BMG, 74321500063, £5.99

Psycho (1960) Universal, 0610433, £5.99, DVD, Columbia, VDR90017, £14.99

Psycho 2 (1983) Universal, 0448063, £7.99

Psycho III (1986) Universal, 0448073, £7.99

Psycho IV - The Beginning (1990) Universal, 0448083, £7.99

The Slayer (1980) Vipco, VIP007, £11.99

The Texas Chainsaw Massacre (1974) Blue Dolphin, BDV2015, £12.99, DVD, BDV001, £17.99

Scream (1997) Buena Vista, D610579, £8.99, DVD, DO34558, £14.99

Scream 2 (1998) Buena Vista, D910541, £8.99, DVD, DO34568, £14.99

(*Scream 3* is most likely to be available in video late 2000)

The Stepfather (1996) Carlton, 3007420553, £6.99

Urban Legend (1998) Columbia Tristar, CVR28311, £10.99, DVD, CDR98311, £14.99

Slash Dot.Com

There are, of course, countless sites dedicated to the discussion of, and the dissection of, the horror movie. Those that have a certain slasher bent include:

Fangoria Magazine Online - http://www.fangoria2000.com - The granddaddy of glossy gore-movie magazines now has reassuringly familiar online presence. Replete with news on up-and-coming horror movies, interviews with genre stars and extracts from the current hardcopy issue hitting the streets. The only disappointment is their search engine, which contains no archive material but checks your film/ actor enquiry against which back issue you need to buy to read the article. Cheapskates.

Losman's Lair Of Horror - http://www.losman.com - This excellent horror film site contains star biographies, various top ten charts and many gruesome stills. Enter the Camp Crystal Lake page for *Friday The 13th* movie reviews or try Slasher City where all the major genre entries are examined, including body-count scores. Nice.

Scarymovies.com - http://www.scarymovies.com - An eye-popping, image-heavy labour of love laden with montages of scenes from classic horror movies. Copious links to related sites are also supplied, plus news, polls and coming horror attractions but the highlight is the gallery, which includes an entire section on slasher-movie posters, many of which you can buy online to decorate your own bad house.

Everything To Do With Halloween - http://www.moviething.com/ halloween - Oddball site devoted to John Carpenter's classic slasher and its less impressive sequels. Supplies lots of information, postcards to download and even games based on the series.

And just in case there were any doubts about further *Scream* sequels, be warned that Miramax have allegedly already registered the domain name for *Scream 10*!

The Essential Library

Enjoy this book? Then try some other titles in the Essential library.

New This Month: **David Cronenberg** by John Costello
Slasher Movies by Mark Whitehead

Also Available:

Film: **Woody Allen** by Martin Fitzgerald
Jane Campion by Ellen Cheshire
Jackie Chan by Michelle Le Blanc & Colin Odell
The Brothers Coen by John Ashbrook & Ellen Cheshire
Film Noir by Paul Duncan
Terry Gilliam by John Ashbrook
Heroic Bloodshed edited by Martin Fitzgerald
Alfred Hitchcock by Paul Duncan
Krzysztof Kieslowski by Monika Maurer
Stanley Kubrick by Paul Duncan
David Lynch by Michelle Le Blanc & Colin Odell
Steve McQueen by Richard Luck
Brian De Palma by John Ashbrook
Sam Peckinpah by Richard Luck
Vampire Films by Michelle Le Blanc & Colin Odell
Orson Welles by Martin Fitzgerald

TV: **Doctor Who** by Mark Campbell
The Simpsons by Peter Mann

Books: **Noir Fiction** by Paul Duncan

Available at all good bookstores at £2.99 each, or send a cheque to: **Pocket Essentials (Dept SM), 18 Coleswood Rd, Harpenden, Herts, AL5 1EQ, UK** Please make cheques payable to 'Oldcastle Books.' Add 50p postage & packing for each book in the UK and £1 elsewhere.

US customers can send $5.95 plus $1.95 postage & packing for each book to **Trafalgar Square Publishing, PO Box 257, Howe Hill Road, North Pomfret, Vermont 05053, USA**. tel: 802-457-1911, fax: 802-457-1913, e-mail: tsquare@sover.net

Customers worldwide can order online at **www.pocketessentials.com**, **www.amazon.com** and at all good online bookstores.